FORTUNE-BUILDING COMMODITY SPREADS

FORTUNE-BUILDING COMMODITY SPREADS

By
Thomas Kallard

Windsor Books, Brightwaters, NY

Published by Windsor Books
P.O. Box 280
Brightwaters, N.Y. 11718

Manufactured in the United States of America

ISBN 0-930233-47-6

CAVEAT: It should be noted that all commodity trades, patterns, charts, systems, etc., discussed in this book are for illustrative purposes only and are not to be construed as specific advisory recommendations. Further note that no method of trading or investing is foolproof or without difficulty, and past performance is no guarantee of future performance. All ideas and material presented are entirely those of the author and do not necessarily reflect those of the publisher or bookseller.

TABLE OF CONTENTS

APPENDIX
    Explanatory notes for spread charts - Contract facts and figures - Spread margin requirements - Key to contract months - Entering a spread order.

PREFACE

Thomas Kallard's work first came to the attention of the trading public in 1974 with the publication of his book, "Make Money In Commodity Spreads." In 1982 a new edition of his book was published, updating the first and incorporating many new markets which began trading since the mid-70's. The 1982 edition was simply titled, "Commodity Spreads." Now, retired from trading, Thomas Kallard has come out with the third and final edition of his spread trading book. Titled, "Fortune-Building Commodity Spreads," Mr. Kallard includes the best "classic" spreads from his earlier works with new spreads in markets which have only begun trading since 1982. Also included are new spread opportunities recently emerging in the more established markets.

The boom in new futures contracts since the early '80s clearly spelled out the need for this updated edition. With the publication of "Fortune-Building Commodity Spreads," Thomas Kallard has provided traders with the necessary spreading information to keep profit levels high well into the 21st Century.

The text is divided as follows:

Part 1 - For those who have never before participated in futures trading, Kallard reviews and defines the basic techniques and underlying theory of the futures market.

Part 2 - A detailed introduction to spread trading.

Part 3 - Presents Kallard's "classic spreads." Spread trading opportunities Mr. Kallard first recommended in earlier editions of this book, which still command attention today because of their high profitmaking potential.

Part 4 - Presents new and updated market spreads and trading opportunities. This section includes a good portion of the updated material Mr. Kallard brings to this new edition. The focus is on new and emerging markets, as well as new spreading "twists" on the more established markets.

- THE PUBLISHER -

FORTUNE-BUILDING COMMODITY SPREADS

WHAT IS A COMMODITY

In the context of this book, a commodity is anything transportable that can be bought and sold. Examples of some of the most frequently traded commodities are: metals, grains, interest rate instruments, the energy complex (gasoline, heating oil, etc.), foodstuffs and, of course, what has been called the ultimate commodity, money itself. Whatever the product, it needs only be transportable and easily divided into standard units.

COMMODITY TRADING

Commodities are traded either on a cash-and-carry basis or on organized commodity exchanges. When traded on an Exchange, contracts for future delivery are made between buyers and sellers.

WHAT IS A COMMODITY FUTURES CONTRACT

The commodity futures contract is a standard agreement to buy and receive, or to sell and deliver at a stated future date, a specific quantity and designated quality of a commodity at an agreed upon price. Note the key words: future date. The contract is designed by an organized commodity exchange. The price is determined by open auction on the Exchange's floor.

FUTURES TRADING

On the early commodity exchanges business was conducted on a cash basis. The Exchange's primary function was to find a buyer and seller to take and make delivery of the actual commodity. Today, fewer than 1% of all futures contracts are settled by delivery. Commercial and speculative traders, both, usually find it advantageous to terminate their contractual obligations by initiating equal but opposite offsetting transactions. A trader who is *long* in wheat, for example, will liquidate his position before the delivery date by selling his contract in the open market. A trader who is *short*, conversely, must buy contracts for the commodity to cover the sales of it he has already made.

Modern commodity exchanges have thus become financial markets where commercial traders buy and sell futures contracts as a means of protection, a *hedge* against the volatility of commodity prices. Speculators on the other hand are attracted by the possibility of profit from this same volatility against which the commercial traders need protection. The speculator profits from price fluctuations when he forecasts them correctly. His profit or loss is determined by the difference in the prices from the time of initiation to the liquidation of his transaction. Brokerage costs must be included; they are an addition to loss and a subtraction from profit.

Speculators are the market's life blood. They provide the liquidity needed to absorb the commercial hedging activity. When a commercial trader sets up a hedge to protect his financial interests, the speculator is on the other side of the transaction where he trusts he has called the right turn on the market's movement. The point, however, is that both the trader and the speculator have achieved their purpose. The mechanics of their transactions are specific and will be gone into later, with dollars and cents examples.

On any commodity exchange one can buy or sell a contract for delivery only in the designated delivery months set by that Exchange. Buying a contract is called taking a *long* position, selling a contract, a *short* position. On most exchanges, trading is confined to a few calendar months each year. In wheat and corn, for example, the designated delivery months are March, May, July, September and December. Although the price is set in the market when the trade is made, the delivery month must be determined before the trade is made.

TRADING UNITS

Although there are over 100 different commodity futures contracts now traded on North American exchanges there is yet no such thing as a typical contract. Wheat, corn, soybeans, for example, are all traded on the Chicago Board of Trade, and each is for 5,000 bushels per contract. Sugar #11, however, on the Coffee, Sugar and Cocoa Exchange is for 112,000 pounds per contract. On the New York Mercantile Exchange No. 2 Heating Oil is for 42,000 gallons. Live Beef Cattle contracts on the Chicago Mercantile Exchange are for 40,000 pounds, and U.S. Treasury Bills, on the same Exchange, are sold in the amount of one million dollars per contract.

When a trader gives his broker an order, therefore, he does not have to say how many pounds, bushels or ounces he wants, only how many contracts and on which Exchange. If he says: "Buy one December gold on the COMEX (Commodity Exchange, Inc.)," the broker understands it is for the Exchange's contract unit of 100 troy ounces. The trader must specify the Exchange, however, because sometimes different Exchanges will have different trading units.

DELIVERY AND DELIVERY MONTH

Delivery is the fulfillment of a futures contract by delivering or by accepting delivery of the actual physical commodity. It is the obligation of the seller (short position) to deliver the commodity as soon as trading officially ceases for a given delivery month. The owner of a contract (long position) may be notified during the expiration month that delivery will be made. If such long position remains open after trading for the delivery month ceases, delivery of the physical commodity will be made.

The owner of a contract who does not want delivery can close out his long position by selling an equivalent contract at any time prior to the close of trading (final trading day) for the delivery month. The trader who is short, with delivery approaching, must buy an equivalent contract in order to offset his obligations.

WHAT IS A COMMODITY EXCHANGE

An Exchange provides the facilities for futures trading. It establishes and enforces trading rules, and collects and disseminates information about the commodities traded. The Exchange is, itself, not in the business of buying or selling commodity futures but is a financial institution licensed by a Federal agency, the Commodity Futures Trading Commission (CFTC). It is set up as a membership organization.

Trading on an Exchange is conducted on the floor, around *rings* or *pits*, by open outcry and by corresponding hand signals. Each ring or pit serves a particular commodity. When an order is placed to buy or sell through one of the member brokers, he, or his agent, executes the order on the Exchange's floor. Trades result from the meeting of bids with offers in a competitive auction.

Every transaction, as well as every bid or offer on which there is a price movement, is fed via computer to price quotation boards on the trading floor. At the same time it is transmitted electronically to offices and quotation boards in every part of the world.

All trades are guaranteed and verified by the Exchange's Clearing House, a service offered by each commodity exchange. The Exchange's clearing house operates much like a bank's clearing house by making it unnecessary for brokers to make daily cash settlements with each other. At the end of every trading day each broker's position, the record of all he has bought and sold, is on file with the clearing house. The C.H. then matches all the day's transactions and acts the role of the opposite party to each of them. It plays seller to every buyer and buyer to every seller. It relieves the original parties to any trade of any obligation to each other, a system which makes for speed and ease of trading.

WHO TRADES FUTURES AND WHY

There are two kinds of traders in the futures markets:

1) Hedgers: Those who use the market as insurance against unforeseen price changes.
2) Speculators: Those who buy or sell for the purpose of making a profit.

Hedgers may be producers, processors, handlers, users or large scale marketers of agricultural or any other commodities. Money managers and exporters also are sometimes hedgers. Hedgers use the futures markets primarily to protect the prices at which they will sell or buy commodities for cash at some future time.

Speculators in the futures market find fertile ground for their activities. When the hedger places his orders, when he, in a manner of speaking, buys insurance, it is usually the speculator who sells him the insurance. Essentially, speculators in the futures market are not the gamblers their title suggests. They, in fact, assume a risk that is already there and their long range effect on the market is to stabilize it.

Hedgers and speculators are essential to each other because the market could not function without the interaction between them. The speculator assumes the hedger's risk by taking the opposite side of the hedging contract. With appropriate long or short positions in the futures market, speculators provide the liquidity necessary for the market to operate efficiently. The speculator, thus, plays a vital role in the conduct of his country's business. He assumes the risk, always present, when goods are marketed in a free economy.

Who are the speculators? In addition to the professional traders, they may be doctors, accountants, lawyers, brokers, engineers, professors, housewives, farmers — people of all kinds. Anyone can play, anyone who is willing to risk his money on his judgment.

HEDGING AS A MANAGEMENT TOOL

Futures exchanges provide a means for the risks inherent in any business to be minimized. By hedging, a business enterprise can take a position in the futures market opposite to the one it holds in the actual commodity. This technique is equally valuable for producers, for users, and for middlemen — people who have no wish to speculate. Their aim is to earn a good return on investment simply by merchandising their products or services. Professional managers, and especially financial managers, now feel that the truest form of speculation is in the failure to hedge.

SELLING HEDGE - FOR PRODUCERS

The purpose of the *selling hedge,* or *short hedge,* is to protect the value of existing inventory. The hedger owns or purchases the actual commodity on the cash market and sells an equivalent quantity of it on the futures market. In this way an adverse price movement in either market will be offset by a favorable one in the other. At worst, it will be only approximately offset because cash and futures prices, while they tend to move up or down together, do not always travel the same distance or at the same speed. For example, a soybean grower might go short by selling contracts in the futures market to protect his commodity against a price decline. Also, visualize a bond dealer who is holding an inventory of bonds for eventual resale to permanent investors. Since the dealer is worried about rising interest rates and the falling bond prices that will result, he creates a short hedge by selling an appropriate number of U.S. Treasury bond futures contracts. If the interest rates go up, the inventory bonds will be sold at a loss, but the gain on the T-bond futures will offset this loss.

BUYING HEDGE - FOR USERS

The *buying hedge* is the purchase of futures to protect an inventory not yet acquired. The buyer (the user of the commodity) hedges against a possible price increase of the physical (cash) commodity prior to its purchase. The buying hedge, also called a *long hedge,* is used by all those in the market who need a steady year-round supply of raw material at a stable price. Grain elevator operators, cattle raisers, manufacturers, and exporters are all long hedgers. Example: a manufacturer of gold jewelry must prepare a catalogue and price sheet months ahead of the selling season. He must know the cost of the gold he will use in his products. Since he knows only the current price of gold, he can protect himself against price increases by purchasing gold futures contracts. As another example: An oil dealer can protect himself against a price increase from his own source of supply by buying fuel oil futures contracts.

Multinational corporations, banks and export/import firms can use both types of hedges when dealing with foreign currencies. Buying and selling hedges could be set up in foreign currency futures to hedge against adverse exchange-rate fluctuations.

THE SPECULATOR

Speculators will purchase futures contracts (go long) when they believe that the price of a commodity will increase. Conversely, they will sell contracts (go short) when they think that prices will decline. This speculative activity often involves taking the opposite side of trades offered by those who are hedging. Speculators, thus, stand between the producers who want maximum price for their production, and the users who want the best price for their products.

TYPES OF SPECULATORS

Most commodity speculators are *position traders*. They study fundamental data as background information and then analyze price history to predict price change. Technical analysis is the position trader's tool, the one they use most to make trading decisions. These speculators take long-term risks because their positions are held for several weeks or months.

The *short-term traders* attempt to profit from intermediate price changes or sudden changes in market psychology. Their positions are usually held for a few days or weeks.

The *day trader* completes all transactions within a single trading day.

The *scalper* trades in the pit where the supply/demand situation changes from moment-to-moment. The scalper makes a multitude of trades with profit margins as small as 1/4 of a cent per trade. His hyperactivity provides additional fluidity to pit trading.

Another type of speculator uses a technique called spreading. The spreader searches for special situations where there are distorted or perhaps abnormal price differences between related commodities . . . or, unusual price differentials between two delivery months of the same commodity . . . or, an unusual relationship between two different commodity markets. A spreader, accordingly, may buy oats and sell corn, or buy Kansas City wheat and sell Chicago wheat. Spread traders simultaneously buy and sell futures contracts of related commodities in the hope that the out-of-line price differentials (spreads) will move back to normal, as they usually do, and thus yield a profit.

To be a successful speculator one must be a successful money manager. Commodity speculation must be approached as a business venture and good business techniques and judgment must be used. Even the most successful speculators are more often wrong than right in their market judgments. When wrong, however, they have the discipline to limit their losses.

Successful speculators pick their spots carefully and concentrate on trends rather than short-term fluctuations. They take the attitude that the market is always right, and try, therefore, to stay in tune with it and follow its direction. When right, they will let their profits run, and may add to them by increasing their positions. Because they stay with a sound trading plan, successful speculators need be right only 30 or 40 percent of the time in order to come out ahead in any twelve month period.

COMMODITY PRICE MOVEMENTS

Commodity exchanges do not set prices. They are free markets in which the forces that affect prices interact in open auction. On the Exchanges, all price-making factors of the moment are translated into a price which is recorded and instantaneously available.

The commodity trader is certain only of uncertainty. The more uncertain prices appear to be, the more the hedger needs the commodity futures markets. The more prices fluctuate, the more attractive the market is to the speculator. The system works.

Generally, the supply and demand for any commodity are the forces that will set its price of the moment. Things like the weather, government policies, acreage under cultivation, carryover stock from previous crops, and domestic usage (among others) will, of course, influence both supply and demand, especially as they apply to agricultural products. Labor relations, national and international politics are additional supply/demand price factors.

The price of any single commodity is influenced somewhat by the overall level of all commodity prices. The awareness of price trends in various commodity groups is helpful in the study of specific commodities.

Some of the long range factors that affect prices are:
* Varying costs of production which cause changes in the price of the final product.
* Population growth which creates more worldwide demand for goods and, in turn, bolsters prices.
* The forces of nature and climate, plus the buying and selling habits of producers and users, often create seasonal price patterns.

8

* Another long range factor which causes the prices of commodities to change is the value of money. As currency declines in value and loses its purchasing power as a result of inflation, commodity prices tend to increase ... since more money has to be used to make a purchase.

In their continuing efforts to maintain an orderly market, the Exchanges have established rules with regard to commodity price fluctuations. These rules apply to both extremes of the price's movement. They state the minimum amount a quoted price may change from one bid or offer to another and also the maximum amount a commodity's price may move, up or down, during any one trading day.

MINIMUM PRICE FLUCTUATIONS

The *minimum price fluctuation* in many commodities is in one-hundredths of a cent. In trading cotton on the New York Cotton Exchange the market fluctuates in points, each *point* being equal to one-hundredth of a cent per pound. Since each contract involves 50,000 lbs. of cotton, each point equals $5 and a price move of a full cent equals $500 per contract. Grains are quoted in eighths of a cent per bushel, with one eighth of a cent the minimum fluctuation in most markets. Since a grain contract calls for 5,000 bushels (Note: There are mini-contracts on the MidAmerica Commodity Exchange for 1,000 bushels) the fluctuation of a full cent in the price of wheat, corn, oats and soybeans equals $50 per contract, and each minimum fluctuation of a 1/4 cent is worth $12.50 per contract.

DAILY PRICE LIMITS

At intervals, news bulletins which tell of crop catastrophes, war scares, etc. appear and are so sensational that the market reacts to them with violent price movements. The d*aily price limit* set by the Exchange for allowable maximum daily fluctuation serves to prevent what might otherwise become a runaway up or down price move. Most Exchanges have formulas for expanded and variable daily price limits for the commodities traded. The formulas are applied after two or three days of limit moves in the same direction for an affected commodity. When expanded limits are put into temporary use, margins, too, are usually increased. When the market settles down, however, the Exchange reverts to its original daily price limitations.

PRICE QUOTATIONS AND HOW TO READ THEM

Most people cannot spend much, if any, time in brokerage offices watching the commodity price quotation boards. They have to obtain the information necessary for trading from other sources. Some subscribe to quote services. Others rely on the print media, such as the Wall Street Journal or Barron's. The following price information is usually furnished:

OPEN - the range of prices at which the first bids and offers were made, or the first transaction completed.

HIGH - the top bid or the top price at which a contract was sold during the day or week.

LOW - the lowest offer or the lowest price at which a contract was sold during the day or week.

CLOSE - the price, or range of prices, in the final moments of trading. Also quoted sometimes is the settlement price which is a figure computed by formula using the range of prices recorded during the final moments of trading.

NET CHANGE - the amount of increase or decrease in price form the previous day's or week's close. Some papers show the previous close from which the reader can calculate the net change.

LIFE-OF-CONTRACT HIGH/LOW - the highest and lowest prices recorded from the first trading day to the present.

VOLUME - is the estimated number of contracts traded for each delivery month during the trading day or week.

OPEN INTEREST - the total number of outstanding long OR short positions (always equal) yet to be liquidated. This figure indicates only one side of each contract since the other side of each open contract is assumed by the Exchange's clearing house.

PRICE FORECASTING

There are systems used to forecast commodity futures prices. The two most popular are: 1) the fundamental and 2) the technical.

The *fundamental system* assumes that prices can be forecast for any commodity by analyzing the constantly changing forces of supply and demand. The *technical system* assumes that if current and past price patterns are analyzed with the help of carefully kept charts, future prices can be forecast. Many successful speculators combine both systems. They use fundamentals to predict long term trends and technical analysis to interpret short term movements. They hope, by this combination, to improve the timing of their transactions.

Speculators constantly study and analyze all the political and economic information that affects price movements. In a given time period prices tend to move in cycles, but any beginning student in economics knows this. *Cyclical price movements* are the norm because many other things move in the same, repetitious way. There are cyclical movements in astronomy, biology, climate and geology, to name just a few. Studying the particular cycles that affect business activity will help the trader to plan his moves.

Business cycles, as they have come to be known, were first given serious study in 1883 by an Englishman, Dr. Hyde Clarke. But even before Clarke, Samuel Bennet, an American, noted that prices, generally, tended to move in rhythmic cycles.

Cyclic analysis shows that between delivery months commodities are subject to a repetitive accumulation/liquidation cycle of approximately 6 1/2 weeks. The duration of seasonal cycles is about 12 months and this is true not only for agricultural but industrial commodities as well. Short-term trading cycles are usually multiples of 6 1/2 weeks, while long-term cycles may last many years. For example, the cycle for hogs is 4 years, 10 years for sugar, 5.9 years for cotton and 9 years for cattle.

Seasonal factors exert an important effect on the price movements of many commodities. Grain prices, for example, often reach their bottoms in the summer when the marketing of wheat and oats reach their peaks. Non-agricultural commodities also show seasonal characteristics and the speculator should be as aware of them as he is that excessive supplies or shortages can offset seasonal influences.

It is unusual for commodity prices to rise during a recession but they tend to do so when inflation lifts the general price level. It is possible, therefore, that prices will move in a contra-seasonal direction, but the seasonal factor is always there and must always be considered. To disregard it makes the odds against successful futures trading that much longer.

CHARTS AND TECHNICAL ANALYSIS

According to fundamental theory, the price of a commodity today reflects all the available information. Analysts, however, who use the technical method for forecasting, believe that markets have dynamic qualities of their own, qualities not dependent on supply and demand but arising from patterns of group behavior.

Technicians use chart analysis in their study of market action. Their working tool is a chart which depicts price movements over a period of time. The forecasting process consists of identifying and interpreting the various configurations of the chart. Technicians have their own jargon. They identify trend lines, support areas, resistance areas, tops and bottoms, head-and-shoulder formations, pennants, flags, triangles, gaps and other recognizable patterns. Many of these patterns appear and re-appear regularly. Once the speculator diagnoses the beginning formation of a pattern, the price objective is calculated on the assumption that future price fluctuations will complete the pattern.

The purpose of chart reading is to measure the relative strength of buying and selling pressures

11

in the market. If, at a given time, buying pressure is more powerful than selling pressure, prices will rise. The reverse, of course, is equally true.

TRADING VOLUME

The trading volume figures reported by the exchanges indicate the number of trades in ALL futures contracts for a particular commodity on a given day. Increasing volume during an uptrend indicates an additional price increase and, similarly, increasing volume during a downtrend will reinforce the price decrease. When a major top or bottom in the market approaches, volume usually expands dramatically.

OPEN INTEREST

Open interest figures are numbers indicating the number of contracts not yet liquidated. Following is an analysis of open interest:

O.I. up & prices up = New buying = Technical strength
O.I. up & prices down = Selling & short hedging = Technically weak.
O.I. down & prices down = Longs are liquidating = Technically strong.
O.I. down & prices up = Shorts are liquidating = Technically weak.

The above shows that the market is technically strong when volume and open interest are moving in the same direction as price.

CONTRARY OPINION

Contrary opinion traders establish positions opposite those prevailing. This system is based on the assumption that once the large traders have established their positions there won't be enough new money flowing into the market to keep the trend going and, therefore, a trend reversal may be expected.

Understand, that chart analysis is not an exact science. Weather developments, unexpected government actions, international developments and wars are only some of the things that can negate price forecasts made on the basis of chart patterns or any other system.

THE COMMODITY TRADING ACCOUNT

Trading is done only between member firms of an exchange. The first step then for the novice trader is to open an account with a broker. It may be either with a large, diversified brokerage house or with a firm dealing exclusively in commodities.

If the would-be commodity trader already has a stockbroker who also handles commodity orders, it will not be necessary to open a new account. The broker will require that the customer sign forms having to do with the internal segregation of funds and also a standard margin agreement. This last agreement binds the customer to make good any losses suffered in the course of trading. Once the forms are signed and the necessary margin funds deposited, the account is ready to go.

The margin deposit is money left in the account to protect the broker against sudden and large price changes in the customer's position. These funds do not earn interest and are used when additional margin is needed for the account. They are also evidence of the customer's good faith.

The cost of trading in commodities is low compared to similar costs in securities trading. On the stock and bond markets brokerage fees depend on the dollar value of each transaction. In commodities, the fees are lower to begin with and only one commission is paid, the round turn one, due when the position is liquidated.

HOW TO SELECT A BROKER

The commodity representative is the person in the brokerage house responsible for handling the customer's account. He accepts the customer's orders and, at the customer's request, provides information and guidance.

When selecting a broker, look for one who:

- Specializes in commodity trading or is at least knowledgeable about it.
- Promises prompt and reliable execution of trades and prompt call-backs on completed trades.
- Has a good commodity research organization behind him, or her.
- Is willing and interested to send you free daily and/or weekly fundamental and technical market letters and special situation reports.
- Is at least conversant with and interested in commodity spread trading - which will be your major area of interest.
- Is willing to discuss the firm's margin requirements for outright as well as spread positions.
- Will quote the brokerage fees for outright and spread positions (Note: there are large differences in the fees charged by full-service brokerage houses as well as among discount brokers.)

MARGINS AND LEVERAGE

When buying or selling a contract, or when setting up a spread, which involves simultaneous buying and selling, a margin deposit must be made. Margin money is required by the Exchanges to bind the broker to the transaction. Margin rates for each commodity are set by the Exchanges on which they are traded. The Exchanges establish the minimum *initial margins,* but individual brokerage houses usually require higher ones. Unlike those on security accounts, which represent an ownership interest for the buyer of the security, margins in commodities do not mean actual ownership. They are instead more like a security deposit, a token of good faith, so called *earnest money.* Commodity margins are amounts deposited by both buyer and seller of futures contracts as an assurance that their contractual commitments will be met.

After the initial margin is deposited and a trade is made, margin equity must be maintained to cover an adverse price change. Besides the initial minimum margins, therefore, the Exchanges also specify m*inimum maintenance* schedules. Let's say the minimum initial margin required by the Exchange is $1,500 for a given contract. The brokerage house may ask for a $2,000 margin deposit with a maintenance margin of $1,500. A price move in excess of $500 against the trader means that the trader must bring the margin deposit back up to $2,000 by depositing the additional funds required. On the other hand, any gain resulting from a favorable price move is credited every day to the trader's account. The profit may be withdrawn from the account at any time or re-invested elsewhere where it will earn interest daily. Many brokerage houses have tie-ins with money market funds and automatically transfer idle funds into them.

Margin requirements are usually 5-15 percent of contract value, but when markets become volatile, margins may be raised substantially. (Note: In low-risk spread positions, the margin required may be less than 5%).

While low margins provide the opportunity to establish large positions on small margin capital, a relatively small adverse price fluctuation can create large losses relative to the capital involved. A $40 stock would require $2,000 to $3,600 margin (50-90% margin) per hundred shares. A move to $50 would result in $1,000 profit to the speculator who is long the stock. The commodity trader who is long one contract of copper at 80¢ per pound may be required to deposit $2,000 in initial margin. If the price of copper moves up by 20¢ to $1.00/lb., the trader would have a profit of $5,000. This large profit (or loss) potential gives the commodity markets the reputation of extreme price volatility.

Let us look at another example: A trader may decide to buy a contract for 5,000 bushels of wheat for $5 per bushel. Initial margin of $1,500 is deposited with the broker and a purchase is made for the trader's account. A 5% increase in the price of wheat to $5.25 ($1,250 gain in contract value) will mean a profit of 80% on the margin deposit after a commission of $50 is paid. The same profit would have been realized by a trader who sold short if the price of wheat decreased by 5%.

5,000 bushels of wheat X $5/bushel = $25,000 contract value.

$25,000 x 0.05 = $1,250 (profit on a 5% increase in price) .

Profit minus commission: $1,250 - $50 = $1,200 net profit.

$1,200 (net profit) ÷ $1,500 (margin) = 80% profit on margin.

If the price moves adversely, the leverage will work against the trader. If this happens, and the trader's maintenance margin level is reached, he will get a call from his broker for additional margin money.

The trader now has two choices:

  (1) Put up more margin money.

  (2) Liquidate the position.

Note this, however: If the trader chooses to liquidate, it may happen that the broker cannot execute the order immediately because of a limit price move by the commodity on that particular day, or a string of limit moves over a period of time. This is unfortunate but, understand, the trader is responsible for the ensuing losses until his position finally is liquidated.

In the past it has not been unusual for many commodity futures contracts to make four or more consecutive daily limit moves. This may help explain why margin requirements have risen. Increased margins not only protect the brokerage house which must settle every day with the Exchange's clearing house, but serve as well to discourage speculators who lack sufficient funds (risk capital). Higher margins also reflect the increased dollar value of the contracts traded.

COMMISSIONS

The single commission charged by the brokerage firm for a futures contract is for the round turn. This includes both the initial and the offsetting trades. Commissions are paid by the trader at the time the contract is closed out.

Commissions vary with the different commodities traded but, in general, they are modest when compared with those charged for transactions in the securities markets. Commissions on futures contracts are negotiable, so shop around. Explore the qualifications of several firms before making a final decision about a brokerage house.

If neither a broker's advice nor his firm's research department is needed, then certainly a discount broker should be chosen. In any event, look for competence in handling orders, availability during market hours, open telephone lines so that orders can be placed any time during the trading day, and coverage during lunch hours or any other times the broker may be away from his desk.

Read immediately and check all confirmations, statements, and other communications from the broker. Get brokerage errors corrected as quickly as possible. Correct erroneous margin calls, missed markets, equity figures, errors in reports, and commission rates, etc. Check everything! Take nothing for granted. People still make mistakes, even with all the sophisticated machinery used in brokerage houses.

TYPES OF ORDERS

Following are types of commodity orders most often used:

Market order. The broker receives an order from the trader to buy or sell *at the market,* without specific instructions regarding price. This type of order should be executed for the customer at the best possible price and as soon as possible after receiving the order.

Limit order. The customer wants to buy or sell *within* a specific time period, or *at a specific price.* Such a limit order can be executed only within the given time limits, or at the specified price, or better. Limit orders may be marked G.T.C. (good-till cancelled). G.T.C. is also known as an *open order.*

Day Order. Unless specific instructions to the contrary are given by the customer all orders are considered day orders by the broker. Day orders not executed during the trading day are automatically cancelled.

Stop Order. This type of order is used to (1) liquidate a position to limit losses, (2) protect profits gained on a position, and (3) initiate new positions. The stop order registered with the broker becomes a market order to sell if prices drop, or to buy if prices rise to a specified point. Your broker cannot be held precisely to a stop order because in fast moving markets the price may jump right over the stop price or drop right through it before the floor broker has a chance to act. Since the stop order becomes a market order only when the stop price has been reached, the eventual purchase may be made at a somewhat higher price, than the order specified (or, conversely, the sale may be at a higher price than the order specified).

The trader should study these various types of orders. They are important money management tools.

An existing open contract is *closed out (liquidated, offset)* when a buyer sells, or a seller buys back the contract. When the transaction is completed, the broker first sends a confirmation and than a P & S memorandum (Purchase & Sale). The latter is a statement of account showing the purchase and selling prices (or selling and purchase prices in case of a short position), the commission charge, and the resulting profit or loss.

HOW TO FIGURE PROFITS AND LOSSES

Let's assume that in May a speculator purchased one contract (100 troy ounces) of December gold at a price of $550 per troy ounce. In July the speculator decided to take profits at $675. A fluctuation of $1 in the market price of gold is equivalent to $100 ($1 x 100 troy ounces). Since the price of gold advanced by $125, the speculator's gross profit came to $12,500 on the transaction. Assuming a commission of $80, the speculator gained $12,420 net profit in the successful trade. Needless to say, if the market had declined by $125, the speculator would have suffered a cash loss of $12,580 including commissions.

To sum up, a speculator's profit or loss is realized in the difference between the price at which the position was initiated and the price at which it was liquidated. In addition to the price differential the transaction costs must be considered. The transaction's costs are the broker's commissions and the *opportunity costs,* these last being the loss of the interest the speculator's money would have earned had it not been used to provide the margin deposit for each contract.

Most people with only stock market experience would use margin money as the basis for figuring profits or losses. In commodity trading this is poor technique. Margin requirements are not actually relevant to profit or loss calculations. Margin money is a surety deposit. It is not a cost, or a measure of value, an investment or a purchase price. Commissions on the other hand, are a real cost and their effect on the profitability of a trade can be substantial.

The success of a trade can be measured by the percentage of profit realized on the amount of funds invested: *the rate of return.*

The rate of return is calculated as follows:

Net Profit divided by *Cost* equals *Rate of Return* (in %).

To determine the *Net Profit,* calculate the gross profit from a trade, then deduct the commission payable, and the interest income lost on the margin deposit while the trade was open. Let us say the sum for margin deposit was withdrawn from a money market fund for the duration of the trade. To determine the *Cost,* we add the interest lost and the commission.

In order for the rate of return figure to be meaningful, it must be calculated on an annual basis. This is done as follows: Once the rate of return has been calculated, multiply this by 52 (weeks). Then divide this amount by the number of weeks it took to complete the transaction, from the time the position was established until it was liquidated. The figure obtained will show the *annualized rate of return.* This then is the formula:

Percentage Rate of Return X 52	÷	Weeks Elapsed During Transaction	=	Annualized Rate Of Return (%)

As an example, take a second look at the gold transaction described at the beginning of this section. The speculator's gross profit was $12,500 and the trade was open for five weeks. Eighty dollars was paid for commission, and margin deposit was set at a very high $15,000, a result of the volatile fluctuations and high price of gold. The margin money was withdrawn for five weeks from a money market fund which at the time yielded 9% annually.

Cost:	Commission	+	Loss of Interest		
	$80	+	$130	=	$210

Gross Profit: $12,500
Minus Costs: _____210_

                            Net Profit: $12,290

Rate of Return:	Net Profit	+	Cost		
	$12,290	÷	$210	=	5,852%

Rate of Return	X	52	÷	Weeks Elapsed	=	Annualized Rate of Return
5,852	X	52	÷	5	=	60,865%

Thus, the true annualized rate of return on this trade is a fantastic sixty thousand percent. But, the trader who put up $15,000 margin to initiate the trade and in five weeks made a net profit of $12,290 will tend to calculate the profit to be 82% ($12,290 + $15,000), and the annualized rate of return as a still hefty 853% (82 x 52 ÷ 5). But from the loser's viewpoint, the $125 upside move against a short position would have created a loss of $12,500 plus commission ($80), plus loss of interest ($130), to add up to a total loss of $12,710, meaning that about 85% of the initial margin would have been wiped out.

ON TRADING

- People read reports on the specifics of supply and demand. They look at charts, consider trendlines and other technical factors. Then, according to their interpretation of the market situation, place a buy or sell order. Their combined actions make prices move. But, even though all the information is available to anyone who wants it, the fact is that very few people act on it in a rational and realistic way. The majority of traders lack emotional control and make their decisions on the basis of mob psychology. They are plagued equally by stubbornness and fear, by greed and embarrassment. These are the losers.
- The novice trader should begin by practice-trading on paper. Actual trading might start in small lots of 1,000 bushels of grain, the so-called mini contracts on the MidAmerican Commodity Exchange.
- Before a trading decision is made, the speculator should always question whether the investment is likely to provide sufficient return to justify the risk. The potential profit should be large, at least 2:1 or 3:1, in relation to risk.
- The speculator should find and then follow the market trend, trade with the market, not against it.
- Attempts to forecast the reversal points of trends is too risky. One should not try to pick market tops or bottoms.

18

- In commodity trading, short and long positions should have equal priority. The trader must be prepared to think bearish, and be ready and willing to change direction quickly.
- Never add to a losing position. Preservation of capital is a key goal in speculation and protective stops should be set at the initiation of the trade.
- The speculator must be prepared to accept several small, successive losses.
- One must use discipline and exercise patience by letting profits run. The possibly smaller number of successful trades will offset the losses, pay the commissions, and on balance, by the end of a 12-month period, leave the speculator with a fair profit.

TRADING PLAN

The speculator must have a trading plan and stay with it. Some things to consider . . .
(1) Carefully select a trade.
(2) Analyze risk/reward potential.
(3) Set loss point and minimum profit objective.
(4) Enter the order, but limit the amount of capital invested in any single trade to a small portion of available risk capital.
(5) If order is filled, make sure the broker has the stop loss order on file. Obtain written confirmation.
(6) If stop-loss profit is reached, make sure the position is liquidated.
(7) If minimum profit objective is reached either liquidate the position or cancel old stop-loss order and enter *trailing stops*. In this way one can keep riding profits until stopped out by a market reversal.
(8) In case of a multi-contract position, consider partial profit taking when the minimum profit objective is reached.
(9) Additions to an initial position should be made only after profits have already been accumulated.
(10) Additional commitments should be in amounts smaller than the initial position. This is called *pyramiding*.

RISK & REWARD

The commodity markets have a history of high volatility. Some traders have made large amounts of money by correctly forecasting and trading the alternating bull and bear markets. Others made some money for a while, only to lose it by sudden trend reversals.

Many investors in securities are aware of the high leverage in commodity futures trading. They understand how this leverage magnifies the already wide price fluctuations and how this, in turn, produces generous profits or heavy losses. Very few conservative investors, however, are prepared to take on the risks associated with the substantial reward potential.

Yet, today's investor also knows he will earn only low single digit returns if funds are allowed to remain in a bank, or in money market funds; and that he will probably achieve comparable returns with stocks, bonds, and other traditional, and conservative investments. So where does that leave you?

One option to consider is an open minded look at the *spread trading method* of commodity speculation. This type of operation offers many profitable trading opportunities and is suitable to today's often frenzied markets.

For the beginning trader/speculator, spread trading in limited risk situations is an ideal way to learn about the market without being subject to an excess of either financial or emotional stress. For the sophisticated speculator, advanced spread trading strategies offer a most satisfying intellectual challenge. The balance of this book will describe spread trading techniques and opportunities in various markets.

SPREAD TRADING
IN COMMODITY MARKETS

WHAT IS A FUTURES SPREAD?

When a commodity trader puts on a spread he simultaneously takes a long position in one futures contract against a short position in another. When he buys July wheat, for example, against the sale of September wheat, or when he buys May corn against the sale of July corn.

The term *straddle* is sometimes used to refer to simultaneous trades in two different markets, like the purchase of July wheat in Chicago against the sale of July wheat in Kansas City; or the purchase of August pork bellies against the sale of August hogs. Another term used to describe these transactions is arbitrage. (Note: In this text I will use the term *spread,* and spread is synonymous with arbitrage and straddle.) When a trader buys May corn and, at the same time, sells July corn, he has a spread position. Although two contracts are involved, one long and one short, the trader is said to have one spread, one May versus July corn spread.

A trader will put on a spread when in his opinion the price difference between the two futures contracts is abnormal. He will establish the spread position in the expectation that the spread difference will eventually widen or narrow and return to normal. When this happens he will liquidate the spread at a profit. Thus, spread traders in futures markets are not necessarily concerned with the up or down price movement in either contract. The profitability of a spread position is determined by changes in the difference (the spread) between the prices of the two futures contracts. The educated trader notes this difference between two related prices and attempts to forecast whether the spread will become wider or narrower. Naturally, the two futures contracts in a spread position must have some economic relationship to each other. If they do not, the trader will have merely a net long position in one contract and a net short position in another. You cannot, for example, spread cattle against copper.

Successful forecasting of spreads requires an analysis of supply and demand along with the many other factors that affect the spread. The U.S. government publishes much material to aid forecasting: situation reports, crop forecasts, foreign agriculture bulletins and others. Additional sources of information include trade journals, financial publications, The Wall Street Journal and Barron's. Brokerage firms and subscription advisory services are also sources for information.

Fundamental analysis will reveal profit opportunities on spread positions. Technical and historical analysis of the spread will help to choose entry points, thus limiting risk and at the same time setting realistic profit objectives.

HOW CAN SPREADS PRODUCE PROFITS?

In the stock and commodities markets a trader profits only if he is right in forecasting the market's direction. If long, for example, the trader profits only if the market goes up; if short, he profits only if it goes down.

In spread trading a trader attempts to position himself so that he will profit within a wide latitude of a price movement in either direction. His profits are produced by having the difference (spread) between the prices of his original positions move in the direction he predicted.

After a spread position is established it, with time, will narrow, widen, or stay the same in line with the fluctuations in the price of the underlying commodity or commodities. This narrowing or widening, or failure to do either will determine the profit or loss of the spread.

Let's look at an example:

During a recent bull market in sugar a trader expected the price of May sugar to rise faster than October sugar. Accordingly, he established the following bull spread:

Bought:	One May sugar contract at 12.00¢
Sold:	One October sugar contract at 12.50¢

Two months later the spread position was liquidated:

Sold:	One May sugar contract at 16.00¢
Bought:	One October sugar contract at 15.75¢

This trader was long in May sugar. He bought it at 12¢ and sold it at 16¢ for a 4¢ profit. At the same time, the trader was short October sugar at 12.50¢. Later, when he liquidated it (bought it back), the price was 15.75¢ and he suffered a loss of 3-1/4¢ per pound. Thus, the net profit on the spread was 3/4¢ per pound. In two months the trader made an $840 profit. The spread margin deposit required by his broker was $600. With the spread technique described, relatively small changes in price will produce attractive profits. This is only one example of how a spread trade can work to produce a profit. Actually, the long May versus short October sugar spread could have become profitable in any of five different ways:

1. The long side (May) rises, the short side (October) rises by less.
2. The long side rises, the short side remains unchanged.
3. The long side remains unchanged, the short side falls.
4. The long side falls, the short side falls further.
5. The long side rises, the short side falls.

These five are examples of bull spreads. As the name implies, they are used in bull markets. More about them later . . . right now the important thing to remember is that, in the example given, the trader profits if the spread narrows; that is, if the difference in price between the contract bought and the contract sold decreases.

WHY TRADE SPREADS?

One reason to consider spreads as a trading method is that margin requirements are usually much smaller for spreads than for outright long or short positions. Sometimes spread margin requirements can be as much as 80% lower (or more). An extreme example was the great silver bull market way back in 1980 when $50,000 was required for an outright long or short position but only $1,500 for a spread. In some commodities the margin requirements are prohibitive. Spreads, however, offer an affordable alternative approach.

A further advantage of spreads is the protection they offer against sudden and sometimes heavy losses from unforeseen economic or political happenings. Since the prices for delivery in different months, or the prices of related commodities, tend to move up or down together, spreading offers protection against extreme price volatility. If a spread trader's long position suffers a sudden unpredictable loss, his short position in the spread will produce a profit of equal magnitude. Matter of fact, when the market is in a panic and trading is frenzied, the value of the spread is usually unchanged because both the long and short components of the spread (i.e. the *legs* of the spread) move the daily permissible limit.

It must be noted that profit opportunities may exist for spreads although the commodity itself is inactive and trendless. Also, with experience, the trader will find there will be times when spreads offer better risk/reward ratios than outright positions.

Experience in spread trading gives insights into market direction and thus is a valuable aid in trading outright positions. The spread trader has the additional advantage of knowingly picking the strongest delivery month for a proposed long position, or the weakest for a short position, and in this way significantly increasing his profit.

LEVERAGE ON SPREADS

At no time should it be inferred that spread trading is altogether risk free, only that the risk in spreads is usually much smaller than in outright positions.

Remember, too, that the reduced risk in spreads is the reason for the much lower margin requirements than those needed for outright positions. As a result of the smaller margins, spreading offers magnified leverage. The successful spreader will realize a greater return on his investment than the net long or short trader provided the same dollar amount is invested. And he will do so with less risk.

CARRYING CHARGES

Adequate supplies of a storable commodity usually cause futures for more distant delivery to be at a premium to the nearby futures. This is a normal market in that the price differential or spread between the futures months reflects the actual costs of owning the commodity for the specified time. These costs include interest, storage, and insurance, of which storage and insurance are fixed costs. The interest costs vary considerably, depending on the price level of the commodity and the interest rate at the time.

CALCULATING CARRY CHARGES

Following is the formula for the calculation of carrying charges:

The current prime interest rate + 1% is multiplied by the market price of the commodity using the price quoted for the nearest delivery month on the board. The result is divided by 12 and then the monthly costs of storage and insurance are added. For example, say the nearest futures contract for wheat is quoted at $4.40 (440¢). Consider the prime rate at 10%: (440 X .11) ÷ 12 = 4.0 plus 4.2¢ for storage and insurance comes to about 8.2¢ per bushel per month as full carrying charges.

Full carrying charges are rarely paid in practice, not even in an extremely bearish market. If the trader is looking at a spread and calculates the maximum price differential between the two contracts will be 15¢, and then initiates the spread at a 9¢ differential, the total risk is limited to 6¢ because the spread cannot widen to more than the full carry, which is 15¢. Thus, the risk is limited to 6¢ but the profit potential is not limited. In a bullish market the spread can continue to narrow, the two contracts can go to even money and the carrying charges then disappear.

INVERTED MARKET

Severe scarcity may cause the nearby futures to be priced at a premium over the deferred more distant futures. This price relationship is referred to as inverse or inverted markets.

In an inverted market, the maximum extent of the spread cannot be defined or calculated because the premium of the nearby contract over the deferred, theoretically, is unlimited. Scarcity causes high prices in both the nearby futures and the cash markets because eager buyers are pressuring reluctant sellers.

THE LIMITED RISK SPREAD

Some spreads are more risky than others. The least risky are those that involve completely storable, seasonally-produced commodities, like the grains, pork bellies and others.

To qualify as a limited risk spread, the transaction must fulfill the following requirements:

(1) A long position taken in a nearby contract against the short sale of a more distant one of the same commodity. The word *nearby* does not refer to the nearest delivery month on the quotation board. It only means that the long position must mature before the contract month in which a short position was taken. Example: A long January versus a short May soybean spread.

(2) The commodity must be one which will be accepted on delivery when the nearby long

contract matures and be eligible for delivery without re-inspection when the deferred contract, which was sold short, matures. Because the cost of carrying the commodity is the basis for calculating the risk involved in a limited risk spread, it is not suggested that the trader accept delivery and carry the actual physical commodity until the more distant delivery month.

(3) The commodity must be physically available for delivery without dependence on transportation.

(4) The short sale in the deferred month should be made at a premium over the price of the nearby long month. This premium should cover a portion of the carrying costs. Since the carrying costs usually limit the amount by which the deferred contract may trade over the nearby contract, the risk exposure is limited and can be calculated.

The cost factors involved in carrying the commodity in storage from one time period to the next include: storage for the entire period, handling, insurance, shrinkage, commission to buy and accept delivery, commission to sell and make delivery and interest on investment.

INTEREST RATES

As shown below, the largest cost is the interest on the money needed to carry the physical commodity from the time it is delivered until it is re-delivered against the deferred month. This cost varies with both the price of the commodity and with the short-term interest rates.

Let's assume that the prime interest rate is 10% per annum, and the price of soybeans is $5 per bushel. The value of a standard 5,000 bushel soybean futures contract is then $25,000. In the case of a January versus May soybean spread, interest on the money for four months amounts to $833.33 or about 16-1/2¢ per bushel. This is a simplified calculation because we would have to pay for the borrowed money over and above the prime lending rate and we would have to add the costs of storage and insurance.

If the trader initiates the spread by selling the May contract at a premium of 10¢ over the cost of the January contract, and buys January beans at $5 and sells short May beans at $5.10, he would have an interest expense of 16-1/2¢ from which he must deduct the 10¢ premium built into the spread when it was initiated. His risk exposure would be about 6-1/2¢ in case the spread widened out to the carrying charges which we calculated as 16-1/2¢ per bushel for the four months.

If, however, at a later date the interest rate climbs to 18%, and the price of soybeans goes up to $8 per bushel, the carrying charges will reach 12¢ per month per bushel, or 48¢ for the Jan/May spread (12¢ x 4 months). Thus, we see that the so-called 'limited risk' spreads do not limit the trader's risk for the whole duration of a spread trade. As interest rates rise and fall so do carrying charges. While falling interest rates benefit limited risk spreaders, a sudden rise in interest rates can destroy the risk limitation expectation that was in effect when the trade was initiated.

The profit potential, on the other hand, is in no way limited. There is no limit to the higher price a nearer month can demand over that of a more distant month. As mentioned before, in a severe shortage situation, theoretically, the possible gain is unlimited.

Some commodities that lend themselves to limited risk spread trading provided the two contract months are in the same crop year are: wheat, corn, oats, soybeans, soybean oil, soybean meal, orange juice, cotton, coffee, cocoa, currencies, T-bonds and T-bills. Pork bellies must involve two contract months of the same calendar year.

Commodities which cannot be carried from one delivery month to another cannot be traded as limited risk spreads. Because of perishability and transportation problems limited risk spreads cannot be established in a number of markets, two of which being cattle and hogs.

CALCULATED RISK

As another example of risk calculation, assume a speculating trader places the following order with his broker:

"Buy March and sell May bellies at 100 points premium for May." The order is filled, March bought at 54.40¢ and May sold at 55.40¢.

The pork belly contract is written for 40,000 pounds. Current price, near month: 54.40¢ per pound. And for the sake of illustration with this example let's assume there's an 18% interest rate:

Contract value: ($.5440 x 40,000) = $21,760
Interest at 18% per annum = $3,916
Interest per month: ($3,916 ÷ 12) = $326.33
Interest from March to May = two months = $652.66
$652.66 is the equivalent of approximately 163 points (1 point = $4.00)
163 points = carrying charges excluding storage and insurance.

When a commercial trader can sell the more distant month at a premium equal to interest on the money required to carry the physical commodity, he will probably be willing to support the price difference (spread) at that point. Thus, the speculating spread trader is taking a calculated risk of 71 points if he establishes a position at a 100 point differential, May over March.

There are conditions under which limited risk spreads may go wrong. All stored commodities must be kept in good condition while in storage. In case of pork bellies, for example, a power blackout could render the bellies in the storage freezer non-deliverable even after conditions are restored to normal. Another circumstance that could hurt the limited risk spread trader is a sudden change by a commodity exchange of the rules regulating trading. The exchange, for example, may decide not to permit the re-tendering of the commodity once a delivery notice is issued. Such action by an exchange, in an effort to cool speculative involvements, would weaken the nearbys while the distant delivery months could go to unusual premiums. Another unusual circumstance is the federal government's imposition of price ceilings on nearby deliveries. While the nearbys would be limited by the ceiling, the distant delivery months could go to very high premiums in anticipation of much higher prices once the price controls are abolished. We live in uncertain times. The limited risk trader must remain ever alert to liquidate the spread once the calculated maximum price difference is - for whatever reason - conclusively violated.

As has been noted, the interest rate and the price of the commodity under consideration are two factors of major importance to the commodity spread trader. Another is the supply/demand situation. If, for example, reduced supplies of hogs and pigs were coupled with strong demand for bellies, the trader might not get a fill on his order to buy March and sell May bellies at May 100 points over the price of the March bellies. The trader must adjust to existing conditions and reconsider the price differential (spread) he is willing to accept when entering the trade. He might have to take a larger risk to obtain the spread he wants but the trade would still be a limited risk spread with a larger loss exposure.

AVERAGING DOWN

A trader dealing in limited risk spreads can average down against a known maximum price difference which is not expected to change or change to the advantage of the trader. There are three such possibilities: 1) Interest rates are holding steady, 2) interest rates appear to be topping out, or 3) interest rates are coming down. Embarking on a trading plan which involves averaging down, the trader will place several *open orders* with his broker.

For example:

1. Buy March & sell May bellies, 75 pts. May over (1 unit)
2. Buy March & sell May bellies, 100 pts. May over (1 unit)
3. Buy March & sell May bellies, 125 pts. May over (2 units)
4. Buy March & sell May bellies, 150 pts. May over (2 units)

Since the trader moves with the ebb-and-flow of the spread, he places a liquidation order with his broker immediately upon a fill. If on trade 1, above, he receives such a fill his next instruction to the broker would be an open order, good-till-cancelled (GTC): "Sell March and buy May bellies, 25 points May over," thus aiming at a 50-point profit. If and when this target is reached, he will take his profits and immediately reinstate his No. 1 open order with the broker. This same method would be followed with trades 2, 3, and 4 if notice of a fill was received from the broker. In trade No. 3, the liquidation order would read: "Sell 2 March and buy 2 May bellies at 75 points May over." This 50-point profit objective was chosen arbitrarily but it is considered a reasonable goal in view of long-term, historical spread charts. Each spread (No. 1 through No. 4) should be treated separately. It is a rule never to break a spread by lifting one leg of it. Orders No. 1 through No. 4 must be placed as spreads and liquidated as spreads.

The trading program above may not be active enough for some traders. It is the greedy, outright position trader, however, who pours huge sums of risk capital into the market in the hope of making quick profits. The well diversified spread trader who has a good trading plan, and realistic profit objectives as part of that plan, stands a good chance of capturing some of the risk capital. The true professionals are those spread traders who stay in business year after year and those with the most capital who control the market by using strategically placed spreads. The small trader can benefit from the big power plays by coat-tailing the ebb-and-flow of this market.

During recent years many spreads have shown frequent changes of substantial size. In the March/May pork belly spread just discussed, the trader took a calculated risk and arbitrarily limited his profits to 50 points per trade. The educated trader, however, can take advantage of a possibly big move by trading an even number of spread positions for each trade.

TWO-UNIT TRADING

In our example, in trades No. 1 and No. 2 he buys two, four, six, or more March contracts (always even numbers) and sells the same number of May belly contracts. In trades No. 3 and No. 4 he doubles the amount. Half the spread positions in each trade are liquidated at the predetermined profit objective of 50 points. The remaining spreads are held for the longer term. If the big move materializes, these contracts are closed out when a protective stop signalling a change in the market is touched.

Often limited risk spreads fluctuate in a very narrow range until the first delivery day approaches. At that time the nearby contracts gain relative to the more distant ones. If this situation develops, the trader, hoping for more profits, will stay with the spread as long as possible. By doing so he may overstay his position and receive delivery on the nearby long position. Should this occur, the trader would instruct his broker to sell, re-tender the commodity and liquidate the short leg of the spread at the same time. The trader, of course, would pay an extra commission, and probably one day's interest and storage would be assessed. While many traders will panic and liquidate before the first delivery day, often large and profitable moves occur between the first delivery and the last trading day. Close contact with one's broker is advisable during this period since deliveries for every day are posted and the broker receives this information each delivery day. If deliveries are small, the spread should be liquidated before trading ceases in the nearby, long contract.

INVERTED MARKETS

Thus far we have looked at normal, so-called carrying charge markets. In periods when a commodity is in short supply the premium will narrow for the contract months. If a true scarcity develops, the carrying charges will disappear and the nearby futures will be priced higher than the deferred futures. This type of price relationship is known as an inverse or inverted market, and involves negative *carrying charges*.

When traders anticipate actual shortages of a commodity, bull-spreads (long nearby vs. short deferred contracts) are very profitable.

TYPES OF SPREADS

There are four major types of spreads:

(1) *INTERDELIVERY SPREADS.* Also called intra-market or intra-commodity spreads. These long and short positions involve two different delivery months of the same commodity on the same exchange. For example, July wheat is spread against December wheat, or May corn against July corn. This is the most common type of spread and includes the limited risk spreads, often referred to as carrying-charge spreads.

(2) *INTERMARKET SPREADS.* The long and short positions involve the same delivery month of the same commodity traded on two different commodity exchanges. For example, Chicago wheat versus Kansas City wheat, or New York silver versus Chicago silver.

(3) *INTERCOMMODITY SPREADS.* Long and short positions between two different but related commodities, usually, but not necessarily for the same delivery months, or on the same exchange. Examples: cattle vs. hogs; corn vs. oats; gold vs. silver.

(4) *COMMODITY VERSUS PRODUCTS SPREADS.* Long and short positions spread between a commodity and the product(s) derived from it. Best known of this type spread is the one between soybeans and its products, soybean oil and soybean meal. Spreads between hogs and pork bellies also are in this category. The spread is for the same or different delivery months on the same exchange.

INTERDELIVERY SPREADS

For seasonally-produced, completely storable commodities (grains, for example) there are three spreading possibilities:

(a) Old crop delivery months spread.
   Example: December '90 against March '91 wheat
(b) Old crop futures against new crop futures.
   Example: May '91 against July '91 wheat
(c) New crop delivery months spread.
   Example: September '91 against December '91 wheat

Spreads (a) and (c) are also called intra-season spreads. Spreads of the (b) type are also known as inter-season or *intercrop* spreads. Types (a) and (c) include the limited-risk spreads also known as carrying-charge spreads, as well as the inverted market situations already described. It is worth repeating here that while discounts rarely reach full carrying charge level in these limited risk situations, the potential clearly exists for the discount to exceed today's carrying charges, because interest rates and/or prices can rise.

Type (b) spread positions between old-crop and new-crop futures are popular with sophisticated speculators. Since different supply-demand conditions apply to each season or crop year, forecasting of future price differentials is more complex. The possibility of wide market fluctuations exposes the trader to more risk in intercrop spreading than it does in transactions of the intra-crop type.

Intercrop spreads are not limited to crops grown in the soil. Pork bellies, for example, show a seasonal response to the production cycle as well as to periods of in-storage and out-of-storage movement. Pork bellies of one crop year cannot be delivered the next crop year. That is, bellies in storage in August and before cannot be delivered against the February contract of the next calendar year. A long August vs. short February pork belly contract spread will not be confined to the limits calculated by full carrying charges. The trader must be aware that the August vs. February belly spread puts him in an unlimited risk position.

Among the popular intercrop spreads are March/July Kansas City wheat; July/November soybeans; July/December cotton.

INTERMARKET SPREADS

When a commodity is traded in two or more futures markets and the contracts call for *par delivery* at different locations, the geographic relationship of futures prices may create intermarket spread opportunities.

Wheat futures, for example, are traded on Exchanges in Chicago, Kansas City and Minneapolis. Wheat prices are lowest in the producing areas and increase as wheat is shipped to deficit areas. Most spreading operations are between Kansas City and Chicago, or between Minneapolis and Chicago. A normal price relationship reflects transportation costs between the two cities and if the spread exceeds transportation costs, the speculator will buy the lower priced contract on one exchange and sell the higher priced contract on the other exchange. If the price relationship returns to normal during the life of the spread, the speculator will obtain a profit equal to the price differential above transportation costs. In this situation the commercial trader has an advantage. He does not have to hope for a return to a normal relationship in the spread because he has a locked in profit. All he needs do is take delivery on the lower priced market, transport the product to the delivery point of the higher priced market and fulfill his obligation by re-delivering against his short position. Thus, any time wheat quotations in Kansas City or Minneapolis are lower than in Chicago and in excess of transportation costs, there will be traders buying contracts in Kansas City and/or Minneapolis and selling short in Chicago.

Transportation costs are one factor in determining the price differences between these markets. Another is the intrinsic value of the class and grade of wheat deliverable at each market. Kansas City wheat futures usually reflect the price of Hard Red Winter wheat. Minneapolis requires delivery of Hard Red Spring Wheat. Chicago wheat futures usually reflect the price of Soft Winter Wheat. Each market thus reflects the price of a different class of wheat. These classes of wheat have different uses which make it difficult to substitute one for the other. The soft wheats are used in quickbreads and cakes. The Hard Red Winter Wheat is used for making bread and rolls and is primarily an export commodity.

The third factor influencing intermarket price spreads between the three wheat futures contracts is the harvest time. Winter wheat, deliverable in Chicago and Kansas City, is harvested in June and July. Spring wheat, deliverable at Minneapolis, is harvested in August and September. Thus, trading in July means dealing in new-crop wheat futures at Chicago and Kansas City, while July will still be an old-crop futures contract in Minneapolis.

To sum up, if a trader believes that price differences are out-of-line between commodities trading in two different cities, he will sell the higher-priced contract and buy the lower-priced one. Popular positions of this type include Chicago versus Kansas City or Minneapolis wheat and New York versus Chicago silver. Note: This type of spread trading does not offer margin advantage and there is no commission advantage either.

INTERCOMMODITY SPREADS

In intercommodity spreads transactions, futures contracts on the same exchange for the same delivery month are spread between two different commodities which substitute for each other in usage.

Example: Corn and oats are both feed grains used to feed livestock and poultry. Their prices are closely related because of their inherent physical and economic relationships. A price change in one of these commodities will directly affect the price of the other. As the price of corn rises relative to the price of oats, the use of oats as livestock feed will increase. Even though oats are usually lower in price than corn, this shift in usage will slow the price rise in corn and increase the price of oats. In order to establish that the price difference between futures contracts of such related commodities is out of line, the price analyst must consider the following: A bushel of oats weighs 32 pounds and corn weighs 56 pounds; a pound of oats has 95% as much feed value for milk cows as corn and 85% as much value for beef cattle and hogs. The trader, therefore, would spread two units of oats against one unit of corn. This compensates for the smaller weight of a bushel of oats and its generally narrower price swings relative to corn.

The price relationship between oats and corn tends to develop a seasonal pattern which must be considered. Seasonal price trends may account for out-of-line price spreads between substitute commodities and result in spreading opportunities for the speculator.

Oats are harvested in July and August; corn is harvested in October and November. Harvest

33

pressure weighs on oats during July and August and may depress oats prices to 50% or less of the price of corn. In this situation the trader will purchase two December oats contracts and sell one December corn contract. While corn is under maximum harvest pressure in November, oats prices, with harvest pressure removed, may strengthen and the price spread between oats and corn will probably return to the realistic level of 60%. The trader will then liquidate the spread and profit by the seasonal change in the price relationships. Since this spread would be initiated in August and held through November, the corn situation should be carefully checked before establishing the spread position. Anything that could hurt new-crop corn production, such as blight, or drought, could result in advancing corn prices. If the new crop situation became serious, the spread differential expected by the speculator would widen instead of narrowing, with, theoretically, no limit to where it would have to stop.

The most popular intercommodity spreads are in the corn and wheat markets. Wheat is used primarily as a food grain, but it can also be used as feed for livestock. A bushel of wheat weighs 7% more than a bushel of corn and, per-pound, wheat has about 5% higher feed value. On this basis, a bushel of wheat should be worth 12% to 13% more than a bushel of corn for livestock feeding. If the price differential is less than 12%, the spread trader will buy wheat and sell corn in anticipation of a widening spread.

Wheat is usually at its lowest price during harvest time. Relatively heavy harvest shipment of Chicago (Soft Red Winter) wheat often results in seasonally low prices in July. Since corn harvest occurs in the fall, July is often the seasonally strong month for corn futures. Speculators establish their spreads in June, going long December wheat versus short December corn. They liquidate the spreads in November or December.

To take advantage of the low price in wheat during the harvest season, speculators take opposite positions: Long December corn against short December wheat, initiating the spread in March and liquidating in June.

The prices of some grains are more volatile than others. An analysis of the supply/demand situation in wheat, corn and soybeans may indicate profitable spread opportunities during seasonal weakness. If there are indications of a relatively small soybean crop, the beans usually show a larger seasonal price advance than wheat or corn. Thus, spreading long soybeans versus short wheat or corn futures could result in highly profitable spread trades.

The largest quantities of corn and soybeans are produced in the corn belt states of Nebraska, Iowa, Illinois, Indiana and Ohio. In these states corn planting starts early in May and is expected to be completed by May 25. Soybeans are planted in the same states during the second half of May. If prior to and during the planting period the ground is too wet to plant, each day of delay in planting is likely to result in a switch of more acreage from corn to soybeans. If a speculator expects soybeans acreage to be increased at the expense of other crops (corn, grain sorghum and cotton), he will sell March (of the next calendar year) soybeans and expect that the spread premium for soybeans will decrease versus corn. Keep in mind, however, that each day corn planting is delayed beyond May 25 will reduce the yield by one bushel per acre.

MONEY SPREADS

In intercommodity spreading it is important to study the price dynamics of the commodities involved. For example, when pork belly futures make a 5¢ per pound move, hogs might move simultaneously but only 2¢ to 3¢ per pound. Due to the unequal size of the contracts traded, a one-cent move in bellies equals $400 per contract, while a one-cent move in hogs is equivalent to $300 per contract. Thus, such spreads cannot be charted in price differentials of so many points but must be charted on a contract-dollar difference basis.

The soybean meal/oil spread must also be judged in terms of money differences. The dollar value of one contract of 100 tons of meal must be compared with the dollar value of one contract of 60,000 pounds of oil.

In the meat market cattle and hogs keep a steady price relationship for a while but then move wide apart with prices based on changed supply/demand conditions. Here again, pound-for-pound differences in futures prices do not give a true picture to the trader who wants to keep track of equity fluctuations.

Let's assume a trader buys cattle at 70¢ per pound and sells hogs at 50¢ per pound. The spread differential based on price would be 2,000 points (1¢ = 100 points), cattle over. If both contracts moved up one penny (+100 points), the spread differential would still be 2,000 points but the spread trade would show a net $100 profit because 1¢ profit on cattle brings $400 and 1¢ loss on the short hogs nets $300, thus the $100 net profit. The correct arithmetic for calculating money spreads is based on the dollar value of each contract.

```
Buy 1 December cattle @ 68.95¢ ($.6895 x 40,000) = $27,580
Sell 1 December hogs @ 48.25¢ ($.4825 x 30,000) =   14,475
                Dollar value differential:          $13,105
```

Two months later the trader decides to close out the spread:

```
SLD 1 December cattle @ 65.95¢ ($.6595 x 40,000) = $26,380
BOT 1 December hogs @ 49.00¢ ($.4900 x 30,000) =   14,700
                                                   $11,680
```

In this example the trader's assessment of the livestock markets was poor. Both the long position in cattle and the short position in hogs showed a loss. The trade resulted in a loss of $1,425 ($13,105 minus $11,680) before commissions.

Unlike the interdelivery spread, there is seldom a commission reduction for spreads involving more than one commodity. The margin on wheat against corn is as it would be for wheat taken alone, the higher outright margin for either. This, of course, is much greater than in the interdelivery spread, where the margin on the spread is less than it would be on only one side. Some

35

typical money spreads include the following commodities: cattle/hogs; feeder cattle/live cattle; gold/silver; bean oil/meal; pork bellies/hogs; bean meal/corn.

RAW MATERIALS VERSUS PRODUCT SPREADS

This intercommodity spread involves the sale or purchase of futures contracts in a basic, raw commodity against the simultaneous opposite purchase or sale of futures contracts in finished products derived from the raw commodity. For example, hogs are spread against pork bellies. The most popular spread of this type involves soybeans and its products, soybean oil and soybean meal. The B.O.M. (beans, oil, meal) spread involves three different futures contracts in related but separate markets. Soybeans also are spread against either product - oil or meal.

THE CONVERSION SPREAD

Soybeans are crushed to manufacture meal and soybean oil. The profit in soybean processing rests on the processor's ability to buy soybeans at less than the combined income from the end products, meal and oil. To minimize the risk of higher soybean prices and lower future product prices, the processor may establish a hedge called a conversion spread (also known as a crush spread) which involves buying soybean futures contracts in anticipation of future need for soybeans and simultaneously selling meal and oil futures contracts. All this is in anticipation of future sales of the manufactured products. The processor is fairly well protected against adverse price fluctuations due to the tendency of cash and futures prices to move in approximately parallel lines.

Regarding the above, all three contracts are traded on the Chicago Board of Trade. The size of the contracts is . . . soybeans: 5,000 bushels, soybean oil: 60,000 pounds and soybean meal: 100 tons. The processor who buys 5,000 bushels of beans against the sale of one contract of oil and of meal can be reasonably sure he has a hedge that will insure a favorable processing margin on futures transactions. This hedge will offset possible losses resulting from unfavorable cash prices at a later date. A large operator will purchase 10 contracts of soybeans against the sale of 12 contracts of meal and 9 contracts of oil. A hedge of this relationship at this volume is closely balanced to the actual production of a processing plant.

Soybean processors want to buy beans at a price that will allow a reasonable profit after selling the oil and meal. To determine the processor's margin, the product value over cost of raw commodity, consider that the processor recovers approximately 48 pounds of meal and 11 pounds of oil from each 60 pound bushel of soybeans processed.

Example (assume prices are as follows):

January soybeans $8.47
January bean meal $250.00
January bean oil ....$.2650 (26 1/2¢)

To find the value of 48 lb. of meal (per bushel of beans), the $250 (per ton) price is divided by 2,000 lb. which gives a price of 12 1/2¢ per lb. The 48 lb. of meal obtained from the crush would have a value of $6.00. A short cut: apply a factor of .024 to the price of meal: $250 x .024 = $6.00.

To find the value of 11 lb. of oil (from one bushel of beans), multiply the price of oil by 11. In our example: .2650 x 11 = $2.92.

The processor's margin is calculated as following:

Value of meal per bushel of beans $6.00
Value of oil per bushel of beans ....<u>2.92</u>
Total value of products............$8.92
Deduct price of soybeans per bushel ....<u>8.47</u>
PROCESSOR'S MARGIN: ......$.45

The calculation shows that the combined value of the products is 45¢ more than the price of beans per bushel but it does not include the cost of processing the beans.

There are times when the processing margin shrinks to where there is no profit in crushing soybeans. When the combined value of the products is below the price of beans (negative margin, or minus conversion) one might expect crushing operations to cease. This rarely happens. Instead, the processor initiates a *reverse conversion* or *reverse crush spread*.

THE REVERSE CONVERSION SPREAD

When the price of soybeans is higher than the combined value of oil and meal, the processor will sell soybeans, buy oil and meal futures, and at the same time, slow down his manufacturing operations. Speculators tend to join the processors in this type of operation. The heavy selling pressure on soybeans futures, combined with the purchase of oil and meal futures, eventually will reverse the price relationship.

In the cash market, meanwhile, the slowdown in crushing operations will tend to reduce demand and weaken soybean prices. It must follow that the decline in manufacturing will lead to reduced oil and meal stocks and result in higher prices for these products. Thus, the cash markets and futures markets work together to create a price readjustment to the point where the processing margin is once again favorable.

SPREAD CLASSIFICATION

All spread positions are variations of the two basic ones: bull market spreads and bear market spreads. The two differ by whether the near month is a long or a short position.

BULL MARKET SPREADS. In a bull, or upward moving market, nearby contract prices will rise more sharply than those of more distant months. The advantageous speculative tactic in a bull market, therefore, is to go long the nearby and short the distant month. The bull market spread is better put on in a carrying charge market, one with a normal price structure. As an example, take long March vs. short May soybeans, when March is selling 15¢ under May and the full carrying charge is calculated to be 35¢. This spread would have a maximum risk of 20¢ or $1,000 per contract if the spread widened to full carry. On the other hand, the spread could narrow considerably . . . not merely to even money, but the nearby March could go to a premium over the distant May.

BEAR MARKET SPREADS. During a bear market the knowledgeable trader will put on the opposite of a bull spread; he will go short the nearby and long the more distant contract month. The spread trader anticipates the nearby price will fall faster than the distant month's price and this will bring about a widening of the spread to yield a profit. Bear spreads must be handled with care. Their profit potential is limited by the carrying charges but the loss potential is unlimited and can skyrocket. If a trader makes a false appraisal of the market and the nearby short rises faster than the distant long position, the spread will continue to narrow. This trader must use a stop-loss order to protect himself in the event he has guessed wrong.

ANALYSIS OF SPREADS

The spread trader must be aware of the five components of spread analysis:

1) LONG TERM PRICE RELATIONSHIPS: Regardless of the price level of the commodity, there is a tendency for spreads to find support and resistance at certain price differentials.

2) FUNDAMENTAL CONSIDERATIONS: Supply/demand data, both historical and current, paint the broad picture.

3) SEASONAL TENDENCIES: Powerful trend factors in the market. Futures markets show seasonal price trends that have recurred 80% or more of the time. Knowledgeable traders have the odds for profit with them because they will not trade against the seasonals, not unless they know of influences equally powerful and contra-seasonal.

4) CURRENT EVENTS: Things will happen in the news which override well established seasonal trends. A trade embargo for example, or a large Soviet or Chinese grain purchase could well be the catalyst for contra-seasonal behavior. A trader must be in close touch with current events, and all the other factors which influence the market.

5) TECHNICAL ANALYSIS: The art of using past market activity to forecast future price action. Current charts for a given spread provide indications of support, resistance and trend. These help the trader to pick entry and exit points, as well as to estimate the risk and profit potentials.

HOW TO READ A SPREAD CHART

Spread charts depict the price relationship between one commodity futures contract and another. The vertical axis of the chart represents the spread value, the price differential in dollars, or cents, or points. The horizontal axis denotes the trading week and month charted. The first contract mentioned in the title of the spread chart is the nearer month. The price difference plotted is the price of the first contract minus the second. For example, December/March '91 in corn means December '90 corn versus March '91 corn. If the chart title referred to a March/December '91 spread, it would represent an entirely different situation: it would then mean a March '91 versus December '91 spread. Remember, when dealing with inter-delivery spreads, that the first contract mentioned informs it is for the nearer month. It says nothing about being the long or the short contract.

In a cattle/hogs inter-commodity spread the dollar value of the hogs contract is deducted from the dollar value of the cattle contract. There are other inter-commodity spreads in which the contracts are different in size and, consequently, the spread charts show the difference between the contract values in dollars. Some examples: soybean meal vs. oil; soybean meal vs corn; gold vs. silver and some intercurrency spreads.

Spreads between different commodities, like those above, are known as *money spreads*. An inter-commodity spread, however, such as wheat vs. corn, is not calculated or charted as a money spread because both the wheat and the corn contracts are the same size, specified for 5,000 bushels. Thus, a one-cent move in either commodity is equal to $50 (5,000 x 1¢ = $50).

When the first contract in the chart title is trading at a discount, the price differential is plotted below the base line of the chart. The base line is zero, or even money. When the first contract given in the chart title is trading at a premium to the second one, the price differential is plotted above the base line. For example, in a July/November soybean spread, July is quoted on a given day at 90¢ over (+90¢) if it sells at a 90¢ premium to November, or 90¢ under (-90¢) if it is selling at a discount of that amount to November.

Equally, a February/August pork belly spread refers not only to the same crop year in bellies but the same calendar year, like February '91 versus August '91 bellies. Aug/Feb bellies, however, would refer to an intercrop spread, such as Aug. '90 versus Feb. '91.

To repeat: For the purpose of chart construction the value of the second contract in the chart title is always deducted from the value of the first. Which is long and which is short will be indicated in the text, which will also inform whether it is a bull or bear spread under consideration and whether it is a limited risk or high risk trade.

HOW TO PLACE SPREAD ORDERS

Market orders, whenever possible, should be avoided. The floor broker, only human, is apt to give away too much in the price negotiation rather than let the commission get away from him. When this happens the fill price is usually more than the trader hoped to spend, and the profit margin thereby less.

Price or limit orders are the most desirable types of spread instructions because although they give the broker some discretion they, at the same time, protect the trader against bad fills.

When using a spread limit order the limits are set, but absolute price levels are not quoted. The order must indicate the delivery months to be purchased and sold, however, as well as the spread between the two contracts.

Example for inter-delivery spread: Buy 2 July '91 soybeans and sell 2 November '91 soybeans; July 90¢ over or less.

Example for inter-commodity spread: Buy 1 May '91 wheat and sell 1 May '91 corn; wheat 170¢ or less over.

Example for inter-market spread: Buy 3 December '91 Kansas City wheat and sell 3 December '91 Chicago wheat; K.C. 30¢ or more under (or, K.C. 30¢ or more discount).

STOP ORDERS FOR SPREADS

Spreads are calculated on a closing price basis and then charted. The charts are used to establish support and resistance levels, trendlines and set loss limiting stops on a 'close only' basis. In this way the many intra-day fluctuations that would stop out an otherwise good trade are ignored. Some Exchanges do not accept 'close only' stops and for these Exchanges the trader's broker should be instructed to place a regular stop-loss order at the chosen level and enter the order a few minutes before the close of trading. If the spread closes on a given trading day at its stop-loss point or beyond, and the broker is unable to liquidate the spread during the last few minutes of the trading day, the spread must be liquidated immediately after the market opens next morning.

TRACKING A SPREAD POSITION

In order to follow a spread position from initiation to liquidation, the trader must set up a uniform and consistent method for bookkeeping. The trader's concern in a spread is the change in its price difference. This difference is given in points or money and always expressed as a positive or negative number.

(a) *POINT SPREADS* involve futures contracts in which the trading units are identical in size, such as the grains which are 5,000 bushels per contract, or 1,000 bushels per mini-contract. A typical inter-delivery spread would be May/July soybeans. Let's say the price difference at initiation of May minus July is minus 9¢. The fact that the differential is a negative number (-9¢) means that the July contract is 9¢ higher priced than the May contract. If the trader initiates a bull spread (long May vs. short July) at -9¢ and a week later the spread narrows to -5¢, the trader has a 4¢ profit. At even money he would have 9¢ profit. If May went to +3¢ premium over July as it would in an inverted market, the profit would come to 12¢ (from -9¢ to +3¢). Another trader, one who misjudged the market, and initiated a bear spread (long the distant July versus short the nearby May) in the above example would show 4¢, 9¢ and 12¢ losses, respectively.

(b) A typical *MONEY SPREAD* involves live cattle versus live hogs. Let's say we buy December cattle at 68¢ and sell short December hogs at 48¢. Keep in mind that the cattle contract is written for 40,000 lbs. while the hogs contract involves only 30,000 lbs. We cannot say that the spread between the two commodities is 20¢ and watch whether it narrows to 19¢ or widens to 21¢. The point is that even if the spread of 20¢ remains unchanged, money could be made or lost on the spread. A one penny move in the cattle contract is worth $400 while the same move in the hog contract is worth only $300. Assume now that the price of cattle and hogs moves parallel, each up by exactly the same amount. At liquidation the spread between the two contracts would still be 20¢. If liquidation were affected at a 10% higher price level, a pound of cattle would be worth 78¢ and a pound of hogs 58¢. But a ten cent rise on the long December cattle means a $4,000 profit while the ten cent loss on the December hogs means a $3,000 loss. A net profit of $1,000 will have been made on this spread trade.

The above example shows that the correct way to calculate money spreads is to take the dollar value of the cattle contract at current price level minus the dollar value of the hogs contract also at current level:

(40,000 lbs. x $.68) - (30,000 lbs. x $.48) = +$12,800

The plus sign indicates that at the time the spread was set up the cattle contract was worth $12,800 more than the hogs contract. Later, when the spread was liquidated, the numbers were:

(40,000 lbs. x $.78) - (30,000 lbs. x $.58) = +$13,800

The net result was a profit of $1,000, less commissions of course.

LIQUIDATING A SPREAD POSITION

Assume that the spread under consideration was moving favorably before the position was initiated. From the beginning the trader must set a strategy for liquidating the position should the spread turn against him. If this happens the trader must attempt to conserve capital and exit at a break-even price, the price at which there is enough profit on the spread to pay for commissions. If that is not possible then the spread should be abandoned at the price differential at which it was initiated, which means, of course, the loss of the roundturn commission. If, after entry, the spread closes against the trader for two consecutive days, it is a general rule to abandon it in order to conserve capital. If the entry point or the timing of the entry proves wrong, losses must be taken quickly, without hesitation.

Should the spread prove profitable - if it goes over the break-even point - it should then be permitted to fluctuate without a protective stop until it reaches 100% profit on margin or falls back to its breakeven price. Either way, the 2-day stop protection mentioned above should be reinstated so as to lock in a sizable profit or avoid an unnecessary loss.

With an inter-commodity spread the price action of the more volatile of the pair must be monitored. A stop-loss should be placed for that one more volatile contract with instructions to the broker, if the stop is hit, that the entire spread should be liquidated immediately.

THE TWO-UNIT TRADING METHOD

Spread trading, a method of minimizing speculative risks in commodity trading, offers, also, a way to take advantage of extreme market swings and temporary market aberrations.

Trading the limited risk spread with the two-unit method is the most conservative way to participate in big market moves. One spread unit is always liquidated at a realistic, predetermined, profit level. As the spread fluctuates, this trading unit may be reinstated, and several round turns made until final liquidation when the nearby future (the long position) approaches maturity. The second trading unit is held for a longer time, waiting for the big move which could occur as the result of crop diseases, weather damage, political decisions, wars, monetary problems, shortages - whatever. Once a major price change occurs, excitement takes over the market and no one can forecast exactly how high it will go. The second trading unit is closed out only when a protective stop is touched which would signal a change in the market's direction. At this point of profit-taking the trader may decide to stand aside, or reverse his spread position by going short the nearby contract and long the distant one. Example: Short March/long July pork belly contracts. But this is now a bear spread with unlimited risk and the trader must protect himself immediately against a crushing loss. He must place a protective stop which will liquidate the bear spread once the old high is surpassed. In a wild market it might be impossible to fill the stop-loss order at the specified price difference, which could be somewhat higher than the previous high. The loss then would be greater than expected.

DYNAMIC SPREADS

At various times in the past, inverted markets have been the rule, the nearer months selling at a premium to the more distant ones. As long as the strong uptrend is intact, bull spreads may be established with the hope of profit from further widening of the spread. Trading on charts is the standard method of determining when to enter into, and when to liquidate, these bull spreads. If the spread is initiated on a news event and does not show a profit within a few days, it should be liquidated. Either the importance of the news item was overestimated, or it was anticipated and already discounted by the market. The change in price difference between delivery months is relatively slow compared to an outright (net long or net short) position, but once a spread trend develops, it is likely to continue. When the bull market ends and the inevitable market reversal occurs, the bull spread should be liquidated. Perhaps a bear spread could be initiated and held until a stop-loss order liquidates the position.

The only truly limited risk spread is an interdelivery spread initiated not too far from the calculated carrying charges, which are the loss-limiting factors. Once the spread moves in the trader's favor, the spread narrows. Eventually the two contracts may trade at even money. Then, if due to severe scarcity there develops a very bullish market, the near month goes to a premium and the market is inverted. A bull spread initiated in an inverted market is still a limited-risk situation because there is a theoretical loss limit set by carrying charges. When the trader enters an inverted market he faces a dynamic situation. Perhaps the market has a long way to go up and the bull spread will be very profitable. On the other hand a market reversal can unwind the inverted market and the trader who initiated his bull spread late in the game will suffer heavy losses. These high risk situations are referred to as dynamic spreads.

Raw materials versus products, two products which are related, competing commodities, different marketing timings, or subsequent crops of the same commodity can be analyzed in each leg of a spread and set up as dynamic spreads.

Dynamic spreading, essentially, is very simple. Fundamental analysis is used to discover the potential for a strong price trend. Once the potential is acknowledged, the trade is set up, either as a bull spread or a bear spread, depending on the anticipated price trend. In this type of transaction the trader must develop the flexibility to reverse spread positions quickly upon a market reversal. He must beware of falling so much in love with his spreads that he is unable to reverse them when it becomes necessary. An unemotional decision and quick action are a trader's best protection.

CLASSIC SPREADS
AND
TRADING OPPORTUNITIES

GRAINS

CORN

The U.S. produces more corn than the total amount from all other countries combined. About 90% of the corn grown in this country is used for fodder, fed by American farmers to hogs, beef and dairy cattle, poultry, and sheep. What remains goes to the corn processing industry or is exported.

The corn crop year begins on October 1 and extends to the following September 30. The month of October is the principal month of harvest. On the supply side of the equation, weather is a major factor with July and August the critical weather months for corn. Since 90% of the corn is used as animal feed, strong demand for meat and meat products (especially cattle) is essential to the demand for corn.

From January to March the price movement is usually flat. The planting period extends from beginning May to mid-June. The upward price move in April, May and June can be attributed to concerns about new crop planting and uncertainty about the size of the total supply. During the fall period, as the size of the new crop becomes known and is harvested, there is usually a strong downturn in the price of corn from the July highs. Active harvesting continues from mid-October to the end of November. The harvest lows in October and November create peak demand for corn. During the winter period prices strengthen from November to January with the post-harvest rally in December the result of heavy commercial buying.

While the strongest influence in grain markets is the growing season, the lack of Great Lakes shipping in winter and the opening of the Lakes in April also exert a strong influence on prices. When the Great Lakes shipping season opens, exports surge. This increased draw on lake terminal stocks during the month of April usually causes the May contract to gain on the July contract.

The above seasonal price movement suggests the following trade:

LONG MAY CORN VS. SHORT JULY CORN

Expected entry into the spread would be late February or beginning March. Suggested entry level: Even money, or July carrying a premium to May. Expected exit: During the last week in April. This is a low risk - low profit trade but it is one of the most consistent seasonal spreads in the corn market.

Also popular with traders is the July versus December corn spread. Both contracts are of the same calendar year. This is an *old crop* versus *new crop* spread and July is the last important old crop futures delivery month. The intercrop spread trades during the new crop's planting and early growth period. It is quite reliable and usually the December contract gains on the July contract from the fall into the spring or summer. The spread is set up as:

SHORT JULY CORN VS. LONG DECEMBER CORN

It is entered about mid-November of the current year but only if December is trading at sharp discount to July. One expects to exit this spread late March or during April of the following year. By late March, December's discount is expected to be much less, or perhaps December will trade at a premium over July and result in a profitable spread trade.

To avoid any misunderstanding here is an example of this spread: Sell July '91 and buy December '91 corn. Initiate this spread about November '90, shortly after the distant December starts trading and liquidate it late March or in April '91.

The above position can be reversed after liquidation of the previous spread.

LONG JULY CORN VS. SHORT DECEMBER CORN

Enter: About mid-April (watch for bottom formation in the spread chart).

Exit: About mid-June.

Seasonal tendencies indicate that old crop July corn tends to gain on new crop December during the second quarter of the year. This tendency is reinforced by the opening of the Great Lakes in April.

Note: The July/December corn spread must be watched carefully during the critical month of December. If the spread is not in a downtrend during December, it is doubtful that a typical seasonal move will develop the following year.

***

The December versus July corn spread is a popular interdelivery spread. Both contracts are of the same crop year. For example December '90 versus July '91.

The price differential (spread) between these contracts reflects:

1) the size of the existing supplies of corn,
2) the near-term demand for corn,
3) available stocks in Chicago and Toledo, and
4) the cost of holding the crop from month-to-month.

SHORT DECEMBER VS. LONG JULY CORN

This spread will be profitable if a large new corn crop is expected, if demand is moderate, and interest rates are high. Since these factors will force corn spreads toward full carrying charges, traders would go long July, shorting December, thus establishing a bear spread. Corn spreads are seasonally weak going into harvest. July corn usually gains on December corn from mid-August until the end of October.

Full carrying costs between December and July (next year) must be calculated and the spread established only if the price differential between contract months traded is 50% or less of full carry. The spread's first objective is to reach 60 to 65% of full carry. The final objective is 70-80% of full carry.

High interest rates increase the cost of holding stocks and work in favor of the bear spread. An early frost scare, rising demand, and low or declining interest rates should be considered negative factors when contemplating this spread.

***

OATS

Like corn, oats is a grain crop and used primarily for fodder. The crop year in the U.S. begins July 1, thus, the July contract represents new crop oats.

Unlike corn which is harvested in the fall, the oats crop is harvested in July. The largest movement of oats to market occurs during August, and seasonally low oats prices reflect this. Because corn is harvested later than oats, harvest pressure weighs on oats during July and August and may depress oats prices relative to corn. In such a situation the trader would buy oats and sell corn short. This trade is based on the premise that after harvest the oats prices will become firmer, while the later corn harvest will weaken corn prices.

Since this spread would be initiated in August and held through November, the corn situation should be carefully checked before establishing the spread position. The following factors must be considered:

a) the total supply of each commodity related to the rate of usage,

b) the stocks at Chicago,

c) anything that could lower new crop corn production, such as corn blight, or a drought. These could cause strongly advancing corn prices.

The seasonal tendency of oats to gain on corn has been consistent: about four in every five seasons.

The trader must remember that a bushel of oats weighs only 32 pounds against 56 pounds for a bushel of corn. Thus, it becomes necessary to spread two units of oats against one of corn, or for still better balance, seven oats contracts against four corn contracts to reflect the greater weight and value of a bushel of corn versus a bushel of oats. The value, as animal feed, is almost the same per pound for either commodity.

An example of this spread: Long two units December oats vs. short one unit December corn. The spread is initiated in mid-August and liquidated in November. A rule of thumb is to buy oats and sell corn when oats sell for less than half the price of one corn. Two units of oats seldom trade beyond 24% over, or 15% under, the value of one unit of corn.

The seasonal nature of the spread offers the trader two spreading opportunities each year:

1) When oats are approaching harvest in July/August and at the same time corn is entering its critical growing phase, the tendency is for corn to gain on oats prior to (or during) the oats harvest.

LONG 1 DECEMBER CORN VS. SHORT 2 DECEMBER OATS

Entry: April/June
Exit: July/August

2) The spread is reversed when the seasonal low is near . . .

LONG 2 DECEMBER OATS VS. SHORT 1 DECEMBER CORN

Entry: About mid-August
Exit: During November

***

WHEAT

Futures contracts are available on several types of wheat grown in the U.S.

Hard Red Winter Wheat is the variety most grown. It is raised in the Southwestern and Western states and traded in Kansas City.

Another type, Soft Red Winter Wheat, is grown largely in the Midwest and traded in Chicago.

Spring wheat is grown in the Plains states and harvested late in the summer. Hard Red Spring Wheat is traded in Minneapolis.

Nearly 80% of U.S. wheat is winter wheat; price-wise the strongest contract months in wheat are December and May, and the weakest is July. The March contract tends to be weak for all grains due to constrictions in shipping (the Lakes are closed) and seasonally heavy livestock marketings also tend to depress the grains in March.

The wheat harvest in May, June and July is responsible mainly for the seasonal lows in the cash market during these months. The futures market, however, often makes its low about a month before the cash market. The wheat futures market reaches its peak usually near the end of the calendar year and then, after some sideways movement, begins to drop again the following February.

MAY VS. JULY CHICAGO WHEAT

A popular spread of the old crop type is May versus July Chicago wheat. Here, the speculator trades on the differences in fundamentals and goes long the old crop May and short the new crop July during the summer months. The spread is held until November or later, and reversed when the May contract begins to lose on July. If a tight supply/demand balance develops it will cause May to be in demand and close above July as the May contract approaches maturity. Note that July Chicago wheat typically gains on the May contract from mid-November to mid-March. To take advantage of this move, the trader goes short May Chicago wheat versus long July Chicago wheat.

One would enter this spread in December and exit in late January or early February. If the spread chart confirms a strong bear trend, the position can be held until March or even April.

Another popular wheat spread is:

SHORT MAY VS. LONG DECEMBER CHICAGO WHEAT

Early in the calendar year December wheat tends to be heavily discounted but it tends to gain on the May contract as the year progresses. Since this is a bear spread, the trader must be alert to bullish news events. It is important to note that even when a bull market develops, the spread tends to collapse before the maturing May contract goes off the boards.

The short May vs. long December Chicago wheat spread is an intercrop spread. Both futures are of the same calendar year. Thus, if both futures mature in '91, the spread would be set up during December '90 and liquidated before the end of April '91.

LONG DECEMBER VS. SHORT MARCH (OR MAY) CHICAGO WHEAT

Both contracts are of the same crop year and, this is, therefore, an interdelivery bull spread. The December contract is of the current year. March, or May, is the next calendar year. Entry should be planned for the end of August and the spread liquidated by mid-December.

Note: In times of booming interest rates, bull spreads tend to widen toward carrying charges. While this spread is, theoretically, a limited-risk spread, the risk is limited by the carrying charges. As a result of interest rate rises, however, carrying charges can increase to the point where farmers will not want to store their grains. This increase in carrying charges is significant for the spread trader; it means that the spread (price differential) can widen further than initially calculated. The December/March spread should be contemplated when:

1) The current spread is a high percentage of the current full carrying charge,
2) Interest rates are high but there are indications they will decline soon,
3) There is the chance of a bull move.

This spread should be protected with a stop-loss order on close-only basis. If the spread deteriorates and the stop is activated, the trader will be out of a small amount of cash and commissions. If a reasonable bull move develops while interest rates come down, the trader can reap large profits with this spread.

***

Wheat provides more opportunities for spread traders than most commodities. In addition to interdelivery and intercrop spreads, already sampled, there are *intermarket* spreads among Chicago, Kansas City and Minneapolis. These last offer trading opportunities when there is unusual variation in the supply and demand of the various types of wheat.

First let's look at Chicago versus Kansas City wheat spreads. Note that Chicago trades Soft Red Winter Wheat while Kansas City trades Hard Red Winter Wheat. Chicago wheat is used domestically; K.C. wheat is used primarily for export. This intermarket spread is volatile but it has a reliable seasonality. In a bull market Chicago will rise faster; in a bear market Chicago will decline faster. However, in extremely bullish or bearish situations, where a string of daily limit moves occur, K.C. may pull away from Chicago because the daily permissible limit price move is 25¢ for K.C. wheat compared to 20¢ for Chicago wheat.

MARCH CHICAGO WHEAT VS. MARCH KANSAS CITY WHEAT

Seasonally, the March Chicago contract tends to gain on K.C. from October through January. This price strength is a combination of seasonal factors plus export activity. The trader must watch soft red wheat (Chicago) exports and the buying patterns of the Russians and Chinese. Also to be considered is the huge amount of soft wheat available from the European Economic Community, a negative factor for Chicago's soft red wheat. Another negative factor is that navigation on the Great Lakes is closed down in late fall and, thus, Chicago is isolated for months from the export market. Note that if the Russians buy more wheat they will purchase hard red wheat used in making bread (traded in K.C.) and not the soft red wheat traded in Chicago and used for crackers and pastry.

JULY CHICAGO WHEAT VS. JULY KANSAS CITY WHEAT

The long July Chicago wheat, short July K.C. wheat spread worked well for several years. When it does not work, the losses are small. In a good year the trader should be able to pick up at least 15¢ in profit. Since two different markets are spread, the broker should be given a discretion of two cents. This will help in putting on and later unwinding (liquidating) the spread. Margin on this, or on any intermarket spread, will probably be charged on one side only (full margin) with full commissions payable on both sides of the spread.

Expected entry: Beginning March.

Projected exit: Second half of June.

CHICAGO VS MINNEAPOLIS WHEAT

Another intermarket spread popular with grain traders is between the Chicago and Minneapolis wheat contracts.

The hard red spring wheat that is traded in Minneapolis is harvested in the late summer and, therefore, tends to lose on Chicago and K.C. wheat futures in the summer. Then Minneapolis tends to gain on the other two from September through next June.

The trader must remember that Minneapolis is a thin market. It is often difficult to set up this spread.

***

51

WHEAT VS CORN SPREADS

The most popular intercommodity spreads are in the corn and wheat markets. The successful spread trader will consider the demand for each commodity in attempting to determine their relative strengths. Although wheat is primarily a food grain, it can also be used as a livestock feed.

A bushel of wheat weighs 7% more than a bushel of corn, and on a per-pound basis wheat has about 5% higher feed value. On this basis alone a bushel of wheat should be worth 12% more than a bushel of corn for livestock feeding. If the price differential is less than 12%, therefore, the spread trader will buy wheat and sell corn in anticipation of a widening price spread. For example, if wheat sells for a premium of 6% over corn, chances are that feed-grain users will switch from corn to wheat in their feed mix. At this price relationship wheat exports can be expected to increase because foreigners can use our wheat either as animal feed or for the production of flour.

A favorite of long-term spread traders has been . . .

DECEMBER CHICAGO WHEAT VS. DECEMBER CORN

Because wheat is harvested in the fall, the trade takes advantage of the tendency for both wheat and corn prices to decline during their respective harvest periods.

The speculator would establish the spread in June, going long December wheat versus short December corn, and liquidate the spread during its anticipated peak in October-November-December.

This spread can be worked from a reverse angle. In the spring, with the summer wheat harvest approaching, the speculator would take advantage of the harvest low price in wheat by taking opposite positions: Long December corn vs. short December wheat. This spread would be initiated in March and liquidated in June.

***

July wheat is the first new crop future of the coming marketing year and July corn is the last important old crop futures month for the current marketing year . . .

JULY CORN VS. JULY CHICAGO WHEAT

In early December a trader should look for an opportunity to buy July corn and sell July Chicago wheat expecting a price move in favor of corn until the end of May or early June.

For this spread the seasonal high occurs often between November and February, while in the past the low has often come in May-June.

The long July corn, short July Chicago wheat spread is not as reliable as the previously described long December wheat versus short December corn spread. When the July/July spread fails to work the losses can be quite heavy.

THE SOYBEAN COMPLEX

SOYBEANS

The world's largest source of edible high-protein meal is the soybean, and the United States produces about 80% of the world's output.

Whole soybeans have little utility on their own; they are processed (crushed) to obtain the primary products, soybean oil and soybean meal. Each bushel of beans yields 47 pounds of meal which is used as a high-protein animal feed, and 11 pounds of oil, a low-cholesterol vegetable oil used in cooking and salad oils.

Illinois and Iowa are the two largest soybean producing states, followed by Indiana, Missouri, Minnesota, and Arkansas. Planting takes place in May and June, and active harvesting occurs in late September or October.

Soybeans follow the classic price pattern of most annual crops, harvest time lows are followed by late season highs. From the harvest lows in September and October, prices tend to rise until April. Note: The bulk of Brazil's harvest is in April. In April and May increased supplies from South America may put pressure on the price of May and July beans. After May, prices tend to peak, the result of uncertainty about the size of the new crop. By July, however, the crop size is known. The three-month period of June, July, and August is an important turning point in the soybeans market. Prices can go in either direction. By August, however, in most years, a reliable bear-trend develops. Prices go down until the peak harvest period in late October. Soybeans, thus, offer excellent opportunities to the spread trader.

***

JULY VS. NOVEMBER SOYBEANS

This spread involves the July contract for the current marketing year which ends August 31, and the November contract for the next marketing year which starts September 1. This intercrop spread, where July represents the last major old crop marketing month and November is the first major new crop marketing month, is dynamic and risky but, potentially, it is a highly rewarding trade.

In the event of a bullish crop year July usually rises to a sizable premium over November. In bearish crop years the July contract drops to a discount to November. When the carryover stocks are tight, as the marketing year ends on August 31 (bullish situation), July goes to a premium over November. When there is a large carryover (bearish situation), it drives July down relative to November. High, or rising interest rates, are bearish for this spread and would result in pressure on July prices relative to November.

When interest rates move in the opposite direction of bean prices, the combined effects on the spread may be offset somewhat. However, a violent swing in interest rates, like a 5% change coupled with a $1.00 per bushel price change of beans in the same direction, would result in a nearly 5¢ per bushel change in the carrying charges per month. For the July/November spread, 4 months in duration, this would mean a 20¢ widening or narrowing of the carrying charges. Thus, the influence of interest rates on these spread relationships makes it mandatory for the trader to practice strict money management discipline. He must do this regardless of supply/demand/carryover and other fundamental considerations in the market.

Since even in very bearish situations, the market rarely reflects more than 80% of full carrying charges, the spread trader can look for limited risk situations in soybeans if interest rates hold firm, especially when a near term drop in interest rates is anticipated.

The July vs. November soybean spread can be set up as a bull as well as a bear spread and be profitable in both instances. The spread is first initiated as:

LONG JULY VS SHORT NOVEMBER SOYBEANS

This bull spread is best initiated during the fourth quarter of the year and liquidated in April or early May. Consideration of this spread should begin early in November. If there is a carrying charge there is then little likelihood of a strong bull market. The trader should try to initiate the spread at even money, or July showing only a few cents premium over November. If July has a large premium, 30¢ or more over November so early in the season, it is a contra-seasonal indication and the spread should not be given further consideration. The spreader should then await such time as the bear spread can be initiated . . .

SHORT JULY VS. LONG NOVEMBER SOYBEANS

This spread is initiated about the end of May and liquidated on the last trading day in June. This spread is quite reliable.

To recapitulate: For July vs. November soybeans there are two key strategies . . .
1) In a normal year, when the seasonal pattern works, the bull spread is first set up. It is then liquidated and reversed to a bear spread.
2) In a contra-seasonal year the bull spread idea is abandoned and only the bear spread is used later in the year.

A somewhat less risky and very reliable trade is . . .

SHORT SEPTEMBER VS. LONG NOVEMBER SOYBEANS

A low risk bear spread. It should be initiated late May or early June. If entered later it should be at a 25¢ - 30¢ premium September or better. It should be terminated mid-September in anticipation of a narrowing of the spread to even money or a premium November.

The September/November spread is a carrying charge spread within the new crop if set up as a bull spread. Let us say this spread stands at two-thirds full carry. In this case . . .

LONG SEPTEMBER VS. SHORT NOVEMBER SOYBEANS

. . . could narrow from these levels during July, August and early September. The narrowing could result from:

   a) adverse growing conditions,
   b) a tightening of the basis, or
   c) an easing of interest rates.

Any one of the above factors could cause the September contract, the first new crop month, to gain on the November.

***

SOYBEAN OIL

In relative strengths and weaknesses, soybean oil seasonal prices closely parallel soybeans. Oil demand, however, tends to be fairly constant during the year and is fairly inelastic in price. The market responds, primarily, to changes in supply.

SHORT DECEMBER VS. LONG MAY SOYBEAN OIL

A bear spread, initiated in early August by selling December (current year) contracts and buying May (next year) contracts. The seasonal highs are often made in August. The average liquidation period is between mid-September and early October when the normal seasonal low period is expected.

LONG SEPTEMBER VS. SHORT DECEMBER SOYBEAN OIL

The September contract tends to gain over the December contract from the beginning of the year until mid-February. In May, however, a sharp reversal occurs. This is a bull spread. Almost every year there is a good runup of September over December oil. The difficulty here is timing.

LONG MARCH VS. SHORT SEPTEMBER SOYBEAN OIL

In this bull spread March tends to gain on September from early November (current year) until the expiration of the March contract (next calendar year). This trade seems to work only if the October high for the spread is superseded soon after the end of the month. If the spread rises to new highs in November, a normal seasonal pattern can be expected. If not, the spread should be liquidated. Often there is a sharp dip in January which can be used to add new spread positions, or to originate the spread if it was not established in late October or early November. Note: the long May vs. short August soybean spread has a similar pattern.

***

SOYBEAN MEAL

Because soybean meal consumption is highly seasonal it offers excellent trading opportunities every year. A number of trades have 80% to 90% reliability and, when bull moves occur in the soybean complex, meal moves right along with beans. Soybean meal is a lower risk alternative to trading soybeans.

Since the price of meal is largely determined by the price of beans, the two price charts are similar in shape or pattern. Soybean charts, however, can act as a leading indicator because soybeans may bottom out seasonally in September, while meal will reach its seasonal low in October. The reason for this time lag is that new crop beans, after being processed, will appear on the market as meal during October. Immediately after the October low in meal there is usually a runup in price because commercial interests (meat producers) buy heavily in the late fall, especially if a cold winter is expected. Here, one must remember that soybean meal is a major ingredient in pig feed. Thus, fewer hogs means less need for meal. Meal, however, is not an important component of cattle feed and a change in the size of the U.S. cattle herd will not be a serious meal price determinant.

LONG JANUARY VS. SHORT MARCH (OR MAY) SOYBEAN MEAL

This is a limited risk spread. In eight of the last eleven years January meal gained on the March or May contract from early October to late December. As mentioned before, strong feed demand in late fall and early winter results in intensive buying and makes the nearer option gain over the deferred one. This spread is also helped by the prospects of the Brazilian crop harvested during our spring, thus possibly depressing the price of the March or May contract.

High and/or increasing interest rates and high bean prices will prevent this spread from working. Low bean prices and decreasing interest rates benefit this spread.

It is important that in September the nearby month, January, sells at a generous discount to the deferred month, March or May. During the month of October the spread usually turns in favor of the January contract. Then, during the months of November and December, there is usually a strong seasonal upmove in the spread. Meaning January meal gains over March or May meal. The spread is usually liquidated mid- or late-December.

Three important notes:
1) If the spread moves according to normal seasonal tendencies, additional spreads may be entered into once the seasonal turning point in October is confirmed.
2) If there is no upward trend change by the end of October, or if the October low has been violated, the traditional seasonal relationship probably will not work during that particular year.
3) The November (!) futures contract must be carefully watched during August-September. If the November contract begins to gain on the deferred contracts it is an advance indication the January/March or January/May spread will work, and the seasonal upmove may begin

in late September or early October. This motivates an early entry into the suggested spread trade.

LONG SEPTEMBER VS. SHORT DECEMBER SOYBEAN MEAL

Another highly seasonal bull spread. The trader buys September and sells December soybean meal late in January. He anticipates that September will gain strongly over December until the month of May when the spread will be liquidated. This spread has shown a tendency during recent years to top out earlier and earlier. The spread chart, therefore, should be watched for topping action during the month of April.

September/December is considered a limited risk spread but it is still volatile and, thus, quite risky. Immediately after the topping action (usually in May) this spread goes into a sharp decline and this prompts high-risk traders to reverse positions. They will sell September meal and buy December meal and close out this bear spread immediately after Labor Day.

This second phase of the September/December spread is not recommended for three reasons:
1) The spread must be constantly monitored.
2) The original bull spread may reach its peak in May, or April, even in March. Thus, an ill timed reversal of the position will cause either sizable losses or sharply diminished profits.
3) If an unexpected bull move develops it can cause September to run up in price against December, causing heavy losses.

To sum up: The trader will try to find limited risk spread opportunities where the nearby meal contract is selling at a large discount to the deferred months. Bean and meal price levels will be considered together with the interest rate trends. Calculation of carrying charges will indicate how limited the risk is for any contemplated spread.

***

OIL VS. MEAL

Seasonal divergences create spreading opportunities within the soybean complex. For example, soybean meal tends to move up in price during the spring, while soybean oil prices remain fairly steady during the same time. This would indicate long meal versus short oil spreads during the early part of the year, and liquidation when meal reaches its seasonal high for the year. Oil/meal spread charts typically show this spread hitting its high during the month of July. Most of the lows come late in August and during September and, on occasion, even in early October.

LONG DECEMBER OIL VS. SHORT DECEMBER MEAL

The trader should establish this spread in July at a premium for meal over oil, as high as possible. The premium of soybean meal is calculated by subtracting the money value of one contract of soybean oil from the money value of one contract of soybean meal. This is an example of a so-called money spread, one in which contract values are compared. In case of this spread, if a $1,000 profit on the trade is made we shall say that the meal contract dropped $1,000 relative to the oil contract, or, that the oil contract gained $1,000 in value relative to the meal contract.

***

MEAL VS. CORN

Both soybean meal and corn are fed to animals. Spreads between meal and corn are calculated on the dollar value of the contracts traded. This is another money spread. In studying these spread charts students of soybean meal versus soybean oil and meal vs. corn spreads found a harmonious recurrence of up and down trends. These cyclic price moves should be examined closely back over a period of 16-20 months and trading ranges established. At the bottom of the price range one would buy meal and sell corn; when the spread rallies to the top of the price range one would buy corn and sell meal.

***

THE REVERSE SOYBEAN CRUSH SPREAD

The reverse soybean crush spread has one of the most consistent and strongest seasonal relationships available to the commodities trader. This *raw material versus products* spread has consistently peaked during the November-December period.

Soybeans are not used until they are processed. This involves crushing the beans and obtaining the by-products, oil and meal. A bushel of soybeans weighs 60 pounds, average. When processed, it will yield about 11 lbs. of crude soybean oil and 48 lbs. of meal. The one pound remaining is waste, lost in processing.

The relatively constant yield relationship makes it possible to calculate cost versus income by using a formula called Gross Processing margin (GPM). The formula is a measurement of the difference between the acquisition cost of the soybeans and the combined value of the processed soybean oil and meal.

For soybean processing to be profitable, the manufactured oil and meal must have a combined sales value higher than the cost of the soybeans plus manufacturing. The existence of futures markets in soybeans, oil and meal gives the soybean processor the opportunity to set up a three-way hedge. This kind of hedging is known as "putting on the crush," or B.O.M. (Bean, Oil, Meal) spreads. To hedge, the soybean processor will buy soybean futures and sell soybean oil and meal futures. Eventually, he will buy beans in the cash market and sell his processed meal and oil, also in the cash market.

At times, the GPM can deteriorate to where there is little or no profit in crushing soybeans. At this point the spread between beans and products is very narrow but is expected to widen, eventually. In such a situation, the speculator would establish a REVERSE CRUSH spread: buy the products and sell the beans.

The reverse crush spread works reliably year after year because:

1) The farmer sells his old crop beans to meet his June and July bills,
2) During the fall newly harvested beans tend to depress soybean prices relative to the soybean products which remain fairly stable in price during the same time,
3) Brazilian soybean supplies decline during the November-February period,
4) Export demand for oil and meal increases prior to the closing of the Great Lakes,
5) Users of animal feed in the U.S. and Europe accumulate contracts for future delivery of feed and thus support the soybean meal futures prices during the Nov. - Feb. period.

The above listed factors usually cause the reverse crush spread to widen, often to widen substantially, in both bull and bear markets.

The reverse crush is quoted at the Chicago Board of Trade as the value of oil and meal converted to cents per bushel of soybeans, minus the price of a bushel of soybeans.

The reverse crush can be done on a one oil, one meal, and one beans contract (1-1-1) basis:

One contract of 5,000 bushels (300,000 lbs.) of beans yields:

55,000	lbs. of oil
240,000	lbs. of meal
5,000	lbs. of waste
300,000	lbs. of soybeans per contract.

Since one futures contract of oil involves 60,000 pounds, and a futures contract of meal involves 100 tons (200,000 lbs.), it is clear that a 1-1-1 spread will not give the correct proportions. For practical purposes, however, it is close enough. A better approximation of the correct proportions is obtained by selling ten contracts of beans and buying nine contracts of oil and 12 contracts of meal. Thus, this well balanced, full reverse crush spread involves a total of 31 futures contracts.

***

LONG JANUARY MEAL & OIL VS. SHORT JANUARY BEANS

This spread should be entered at any time after the beginning of June at 30¢ or below, premium products. It would be ideal to enter it at 20¢ and below. If it is impossible to enter the spread at these levels, try to place the reverse crush with the products selling at less than 35¢ over the beans. This should be done, if possible, no later than the first week of September. Risk should be limited to 20¢ from the entry point. The spread should be liquidated late in November or early in December.

SOYBEANS VS. CORN OR WHEAT

Some grains are more volatile in price action than others. Soybeans usually show a larger seasonal price advance than wheat and corn. Thus, spreading long soybeans against short wheat or corn futures can result in highly profitable spread trades during bullishness in grains. An analysis of the supply/demand situation of wheat, corn and beans may indicate profitable spread opportunities also during seasonal weakness.

The largest quantity of both corn and soybeans is produced in the Corn Belt states; Iowa, Illinois, Minnesota, Indiana, Nebraska, Ohio, Missouri and South Dakota. There, the corn planting starts early in May and is expected to be completed by May 25. Soybeans are planted during the second half of May in the same states. If prior to and during the planting period the ground is too wet to plant, each day of delay in planting is likely to result in a switch of more acreage from corn to soybeans. If the speculator expects soybean acreage to be increased at the expense of other crops such as corn, cotton, and grain sorghum, he will buy March corn and sell March soybeans (both of next calendar year) as an example, expecting the spread premium for soybeans to decrease. This spread would be initiated between June 1 and July 15 (current year). One additional factor to keep in mind is that each day corn planting is delayed beyond May 25, the yield will be reduced by one bushel per acre.

LIVESTOCK & MEATS

LIVE CATTLE

Live cattle is not a carrying charge market since, by definition, it is a non-storable commodity. Cattle, ready for marketing in February, cannot be carried into April; the two, thus, are separate entities. Despite the fact cattle are marketed throughout the year, there are seasonal periods during which consistent profit opportunities offer themselves. Cattle slaughter and cattle prices vary inversely with each other. Slaughter tends to be greatest in the fall and early winter when prices are low, and least in mid-winter and late spring with higher prices. Before entering a seasonal trade, the trader should look for counter-seasonal indications. He must consider not only the yearly seasonals but the longer term factors of herd building, marketing and liquidation. These are known as the cattle cycle. The cycle lasts for about nine years and is independent of agricultural and economic cycles.

Because most calves are born within 45 days of April 1, and weaned within 45 days of October 1, there is good reason to assume that slaughter will have some tendency to peak in October and be at its lowest in February. All other factors being equal, February cattle tends to gain on deferred contracts from November through January. June and August cattle tend to lose on later options in March and April, but they reverse and gain into the summer.

Seasonally, July is the strongest of the cattle delivery months and February is the second strongest. The December contract is usually stronger than October but weaker than the February contract. The April contract is also weaker than February but may show sudden strength near its expiration date.

LONG JUNE VS. SHORT OCTOBER CATTLE

This is one of the most reliable spreads in the cattle market. One seasonal pattern is for the June cattle contract to gain on October cattle from mid-January until mid-May. When the current cattle market is bullish and the nine-year cattle cycle is in its upward phase, this bull spread can be very profitable by June going to substantial premium versus the October contract; substantial meaning several hundred points. Even when the longer cycle is in its declining phase, June may achieve 100 to 200 points premium. If the spread can be initiated with October at a premium, the trader may look forward to a profitable trade provided supplies are not abnormally large. A milder-than-average winter may cause heavy marketings of cattle in January-February, and bring counter-seasonal lows at this time of the year. With all the caveats, the long June vs. short October cattle spread, when initiated during the first quarter of the year, has high reliability and should be a part of every spread trading program. Once the spread moves in the expected direction and June gains 150-200 points, the prudent trader will use money management stops to lock in his profits. Due to seasonal, counter-seasonal and longer term cyclical cross currents in the market, traders often begin to put on this spread during January and add to the position on a scale-down basis in anticipation of the seasonal low during the first quarter.

***

SHORT OCTOBER VS. LONG DECEMBER CATTLE

While similar to the above June/October (or, June/December) spread, this one is not as consistent. This bear spread should be put on early in August if October trades at 50 points or more premium over December. It should be liquidated during the second or third week of September, as the October contract approaches maturity. Several times December has reached 200+ points premium, but conservative traders should begin (at least partial) profit taking when December trades 100 points or more over October. The price collapse of the October cattle contract usually begins in mid-August.

***

SHORT DECEMBER VS. LONG FEBRUARY CATTLE

When the statistical situation is bearish, it will keep the December contract from gaining too much on the next year's February contract. This bear spread would be initiated in the fall with at least 25 points December premium, and added to on a scale-up basis every 25 points. December cattle usually weakens sharply as it approaches expiration and a 150-200 point December discount is not unusual.

***

THE DECEMBER VS. APRIL CATTLE SPREADS

Traders sometimes play this relationship first as a bull and then as a bear spread. They carefully watch the spread chart between February and mid-July. If the April contract is between 100 and 300 (or more) points premium over December and a trend reversal is indicated by the chart, they will buy December and sell April. The trend change means that the spread broke out in favor of December. As prices move upward December can peak at 200-300 points premium by the end of August. Then, if there is another trend reversal, the trader will buy April cattle of next year and sell December cattle of current year. This second spread, a bear spread, shows fairly good seasonal tendency.

***

FEEDER CATTLE

Feeder cattle prices reach their seasonal lows during the October-November period. By December prices begin to rise, and tend to rise through February and into April.

The feeder cattle inter-delivery spreads have a similar pattern to those of live cattle, but traders prefer the more liquid live cattle market for inter-delivery spreading. (Note: Live cattle is often called finished cattle or fat cattle.)

Frequently, however, feeders are spread against fat cattle. It takes a little more than five months to mature a feeder steer from the feeder cattle delivery date until it is deliverable against the live cattle contract. The most popular inter-market feeder vs. fat cattle spreads are:

(a) Long May feeder cattle vs. short October fat cattle,

(b) Short October feeders vs. short April (next) fat cattle,

(c) Long November feeders vs. short April (next) fat cattle.

Seasonal strength in the spring is used to initiate (b); (a) is initiated during the period of weakness of meats in the early winter.

***

HOGS

The cost of feeding is important in raising hogs for the marketplace. Since corn is the primary feed for hogs, the majority of hog production in the U.S. is centered in the Corn Belt states.

With pork, both supply and demand follow highly seasonal patterns. On the supply side, most of the farrowings (pig births) tend to occur during March, April and May. Since it takes about five to seven months to fatten the pigs for slaughter, the 'spring pigs' are brought to market between August and December. Then there is a shortage of births during December, January and February and, because of this, there is a shortage of production during the summer when demand for pork tends to be at its highest for the year. From the above we can see that the lowest hog prices tend to occur between August and December. In the December to February period we may see transition of weakness to modest strength. But then, in March, hog prices may drop as a result of marketing those hogs which farrowed the previous fall. The month of April is often weak due to pre-planting marketing: farmers dump their excess hogs into the market before they start field work. May, June and July is the strongest period for hog futures because supply is low and demand for processed luncheon meat and bacon is high. Prices may slip at the time of the June Pig Crop Report. The month of October is weak due to pre-harvest marketings. December is the month of transition from weakness to strength.

Many analysts rely on what is known as the hog/corn ratio to predict the direction in which hog production is heading. The hog/corn ratio is computed by dividing the price of 100 lbs. of live hogs by the price of a bushel of corn. The ratio tells us how many bushels of corn at Omaha could be bought for 100 lbs. of hogs, but it does not represent the number of bushels of corn it takes to produce 100 lbs. of pork. When the hog/corn ratio is higher than usual, hog feeding is more profitable than usual and farmers respond by breeding and feeding more hogs. When the hog/corn ratio is lower than usual, the opposite holds true. Low ratios (below 14) suggest narrow profit margins and low future production. High ratios indicate higher profits and greater future production. As an example, if the price of live hogs is $42 per hundredweight and the price of corn

66

is $2.62 per bushel, the hog/corn ratio would be: 42 ÷ 2.62 = 16. In other words, if the ratio drops below 14, the break-even point, many farmers believe that it is to their advantage to sell their corn rather than to feed it to hogs. Thus, we see how a high hog/corn ratio promotes herd expansion. Here it must be mentioned that non-feed costs, such as interest rates, fluctuate and can become quite expensive. This fact increases the necessity of having a high hog/corn ratio as an incentive for hog producers to withhold breeding stock to expand farrowings.

As a rule, ten months is considered the lead time for production of hogs, since a pig's gestation period is approximately 112 days and it takes about six months on feed to bring hogs to slaughter weight. A monthly chart of the hog/corn ratio can be a useful tool for price forecasting. In view of the ten-month lead time, when the hog/corn ratio chart peaks, one expects hog prices to bottom ten months later. And when the ratio chart bottoms, one looks for hog prices to peak ten months in the future.

When the hog/corn ratio is high above the break-even figure of 14, most farmers will come to the conclusion there is money to be made in raising hogs. As a result, an expansion in hog production occurs. Increased hog production eventually depresses the price of hogs. But all this is many months away. Meanwhile, the spread trader must keep in mind that when the farmer decides to expand his herd, he will have to be holding back hogs from the market to retain them for breeding. Since market supplies will be reduced temporarily, the farmers' decision to expand hog numbers will actually turn out to be bullish for nearby futures contracts.

SHORT APRIL VS. LONG JULY HOGS

This is one of the most reliable hog spreads. It is a bear spread and is entered into before mid-February. Most likely exit is between late March and the first few days of April. The spread reflects the consistent tendency of summer hogs (July futures) to gain on spring hogs (April futures). It should be initiated at less than 150 points premium July, with the expectation of closing out with at least 200-300+ points premium July.

***

LONG JUNE VS. SHORT OCTOBER HOGS

This bull spread is expected to benefit from rising prices due to high demand/lower marketings as June draws near. It should be initiated between mid-February and the end of March and liquidated during mid-May. June should have no more than 50 points premium at entry, preferably less, and if the spread is available with an October premium (meaning June dips below October) extra positions should be added to those already established. Expected profitability: 200-300 points premium June.

***

LONG JULY VS SHORT DECEMBER HOGS

Similar to the previous spread. Seasonally, because of the low slaughter, July is one of the strongest months in both the cash and futures markets. Enter the spread after the March Hogs and Pig Report and liquidate this bull spread beginning July.

***

LONG FEBRUARY VS. SHORT APRIL HOGS

Hog supplies are reduced during the early winter months because of lower farrowings during the hottest part of the summer.

February hogs are expected to gain on April hogs into the new year. These spreads are established late in October and liquidated at the end of January.

***

LIVE CATTLE VS. LIVE HOGS

Notes:
1) A balanced 'money spread' exists here by trading four hog contracts against 3 cattle contracts.
2) Cattle versus hog spreads are volatile and must be watched carefully.
3) The price relationship between cattle and hogs is dependent on both meat production and current economic conditions. For example, in recessionary times when spendable income declines consumers purchase more pork than beef products.
4) An upward price trend in grains tends to strengthen hog prices relative to cattle prices. Seasonally, corn and soybeans begin price uptrends in February-March and continue until late spring or early summer.

***

The cattle/hogs inter-commodity spreads are popular on the Chicago Mercantile Exchange. The most popular combinations match up with seasonal cycles: Feb/Feb, June/June, and Oct/Oct.

For example, one expects June cattle to gain on June hogs during the first quarter of the year because of the larger cattle cycle. In turn this leads to expectations of strength in cattle relative to hogs in the spring. This type of seasonal consideration may be overshadowed by technical and fundamental factors and inflation.

***

PORK BELLIES

The term 'pork belly' refers to uncured bacon which comes from the underside of the hog. Because pork bellies are a by-product of hogs, the size of the pig crop and the pattern of the hog slaughter tend to dictate bellies prices, especially since the demand for bellies remains relatively unresponsive to price changes. Pork bellies are used primarily in the manufacture of bacon.

The pork bellies market is the sole carrying charge market in the meats futures complex. Unlike hogs, which are perishable and brought to market soon after they reach slaughter weight, pork bellies are frozen and placed in storage. The "Monthly Cold Storage Reports" are important to traders because the amount of bellies stored and the changes in stored stocks are important indicators of price changes.

Storage stocks are determined by the rate of slaughter and by consumption. The peak period of fresh pork bellies production is late fall and early winter, from October to December. It falls to a minimum during June, July and August. This pattern of production is the result of the seasonal pattern of hog farrowing. Thus, storage stocks tend to increase during the winter and reach a peak early in May. From May through September the slaughter rate diminishes and stocks are drawn down during the summer. In general, bellies prices will peak between July and September as stocks are being drawn out of storage at an increasing rate. Storage figures thus become important to the trader late in the crop year.

As we know, carrying charges have three main components: the costs of storage, insurance and money. Since the contract is for frozen, not fresh, pork bellies, significant storage costs are involved, particularly in view of high energy costs. The trader must keep in mind, therefore, that when pork belly prices are increasing and/or interest rates are static or going higher, the carrying charge would expand - and vice versa.

Pork bellies, like other meats, have strong and weak months. February and July are the strong months; March is the weakest.

Note: Be aware that, while frozen, bellies may remain in storage for as long as eight months; this applies only to a specific calendar year by contract definition.

Bellies placed in storage before November 1 cannot be delivered against the following year's futures contracts.

***

FEBRUARY VS. MAY PORK BELLIES

The chart of this spread usually exhibits sideways movement or bottoming action until August-September. This is the time to establish long February vs. short May pork bellies bull spreads. The trader should calculate the full carrying charge and then, starting at better than 50% of full carry, initiate a position and add to the position on a scale-down basis. These units would all be limited risk spreads, the risk being limited by the full carrying charge. Limited risk opportunities are rare and of short duration and the trader looking for these opportunities must repeatedly re-calculate full carrying charges at the then current interest rates and futures prices. Let us say the trader was unable to initiate the Feb/May spread at 50% full carry, and add to his position at 60% and 75% full carry. Chances are that in August or September the February contract begins to gain over the May. If the bull move develops it is usually of short duration and the trader will gain perhaps 75-150 points per spread.

By mid-October the February contract will probably show signs of weakening and this trend change is a signal to the trader to take the other side by back-spreading: go long May and short February bellies. This is now a bear spread and it has been found reliable over the years because the February contract has the tendency to go off the board weak relative to May or to the other deferred contract months. The trader must watch the spread in mid-November because the February contract tends to be strong for a week or two. If no contraseasonal trend develops, the bear spreads are held until late January when they are finally liquidated. All bear spreads should carry stop loss protection because they are not limited risk situations.

***

MARCH VS. JULY PORK BELLIES

Similar to February/May bellies this spread can also be set up as a bull spread in August, held for a September-October runup and then reversed to a bear spread. Again, there is the possibility of a seasonal up-move in mid-November, followed by a gradual weakening of the March contract in terms of July until the spread is liquidated in February.

***

AUGUST VS. FEBRUARY PORK BELLIES

The old crop/new crop spread between July or August of one year and the February contract of the following year represents an extremely high risk position. Even though the component parts of this spread are only six months apart, there is no direct relationship between the two crop years because, by contract rules, old crop (August) bellies are not eligible for delivery against the new crop (February) futures contract. In other words, each crop year must be treated and analyzed as a separate entity.

***

FEBRUARY PORK BELLIES VS. FEBRUARY HOGS

For balance purposes these spreads should consist of three bellies against four hogs. Reason: a one cent move in bellies is worth $400 while the same one cent move in hogs is worth only $300.

70

In the past, pork bellies often traded at premiums of more than twice the price of hogs. Then, in the late 70's, the picture changed. There were large storage stocks, high interest rates and adverse publicity relative to bacon; its cholesterol content and the preservatives used in its preparation were the reasons for the weakness of bellies relative to hogs. The price ratio collapsed so sharply that for the first time bellies dropped to several cents discount to hogs.

Therefore, it seems there is not any true correlation between bellies and hogs. The trader may take two factors into consideration:

1. Bellies are the 'leader' in this spread, that is, in a bull market belly prices will move up faster than hog prices and the spread will widen. In bear markets the spread will narrow since belly prices will decrease more relative to hogs.

2. A seasonal pattern seems to have evolved: February bellies tend to lose to February hogs from August/September until November/December, then reverse to strength in February bellies versus weakness in February hogs. This relationship seems to last until mid-January.

***

JULY PORK BELLIES VS. JULY HOGS

This is another popular inter-market spread with high risk and high profit potential. The hogs contract has a seasonal tendency to gain on the July bellies contract during the April/June quarter. Whenever the price of July bellies approaches the price of July hogs take advantage of this opportunity by buying the July bellies and selling the July hogs.

Pork bellies versus hogs charts show wide amplitude in the up and down fluctuations. Many who trade this inter-market spread ignore trends and whatever seasonality there is but keep an eye on the spread chart. When the bellies vs. hogs spread trades near the historical lows they go long bellies and sell hogs in anticipation that on rallies they can take several 4-5¢ profits while limiting losses with 2¢ stops on these trades.

FOODSTUFFS

COCOA

The crop year for cocoa extends from October through the following September. Cocoa is harvested in two main periods: The first, from October to March, is called the main crop and accounts for 80% of the world's output. The second, the mid-crop, is harvested later, usually in May and June. It is interesting that, in Brazil, the mid-crop is larger than the main crop. Another fact to be kept in mind is that it takes four years before a cocoa tree will bear fruit. A single season of inclement weather, therefore, can affect the crop for a number of years.

As a result of heavy harvesting, cocoa prices tend to be depressed between November and March. This, also, is the period when manufacturers do the bulk of their buying. The first six months of the calendar year are influenced by predictions of crop conditions in West Africa. By September the crop facts are known. This knowledge and the fact that the harvest in Brazil is completed, combine to bring about lower prices in September.

Fall is the time when manufacturers process the cocoa beans. Since fall is also the time of heaviest grindings and the processors already have purchased the beans they need, autumn is a time of lower prices. There are two periods the trader must watch carefully:

1) During the summer months there often is a sharp runup in prices while the market discounts the fall grindings,

2) A sudden price increase during October/November due to lack of information about the main crop size.

November seems to be the swing month: cocoa either begins to make its up-side move or collapses.

Cocoa prices, traditionally, have been quoted in cents per pound. To convert \$/metric ton to ¢/lb., divide the metric figure by 22.05. For example, a price of \$2,145/metric ton is equivalent to 2,145 divided by 22.05, or 97.28¢/pound. To convert ¢/lb. to dollars/metric ton, one has to multiply the figure in cents by 22.05. Note: Each drop of \$100 per metric ton produces an equity dip of \$1,000.

***

LONG DECEMBER VS. SHORT MAY COCOA

This is a fairly reliable bull spread. It should be initiated in early May (current year) by buying December (current year) cocoa and selling May (next year) cocoa. If seasonal factors work as expected, December cocoa will gain over May cocoa until 4-6 weeks before December expires.

***

LONG JULY VS. SHORT DECEMBER COCOA

Cocoa highs are often made in June/July, while lows are made in December. The long July/ short December cocoa bull spread is another reliable, though high risk, spread. It should be considered in April/May, and if initiated, it should be liquidated late in June.

***

COFFEE "C"

Coffee is grown everywhere in the world and is always being harvested somewhere, so there is not much of a seasonal variation in coffee prices. The trader should remember, however, that while it is easy to store green coffee beans, it is not a carrying charge commodity.

The seasonal decline (if any) during February/March can be attributed to increased supplies form the harvest in Latin America. The frost season in Brazil is May 30 to September 15. The frosts mean little to actual coffee production, but almost every season there are several freeze scares which lead to firmer prices during this period. Once the worry over crop damage abates, the price decline continues from July through September with a possible upswing late in September, the result of pre-winter high consumption levels. From October through February prices are likely to move upward.

***

LONG SEPTEMBER VS. SHORT DECEMBER COFFEE

If world stocks of coffee are low and consumption figures are bullish, these two factors should increase any upward price move resulting from weather scares. This bull spread should be initiated during the March/May lows and liquidated during the July/August highs.

***

LONG DECEMBER VS. SHORT MARCH COFFEE

This bull spread, and the previous one, should be set up, if possible, whenever the deferred contract trades with a premium of at least 100 points over the nearby contract. When coffee prices move up sharply the spread will invert and the nearby contract often will trade for a substantial premium over the deferred contract. Several times in the past the nearby's premium has reached two thousand points.

***

ORANGE JUICE

Because frozen concentrated orange juice is available throughout the year, orange juice does not suffer harvest lows. Seasonal lows are seen from June through September and seasonal highs are expected from November through January. Orange juice becomes a weather market each fall and winter due to the freeze scare season which extends from December through early March.

Freeze scares in mid-January to mid-February have been particularly profitable for orange juice traders. In March, April, and May, the danger of severe frost in Florida recedes and prices reach their lows. The main harvest begins in April and the price soon begins to climb in response to summer demand. Demand remains high into the fall and prices remain firm or climb sharply if traders predict a decreased orange crop, or if an early freeze is anticipated. Under these circumstances orange juice prices may skyrocket by October.

The cold storage inventories tend to be lowest at the end of the crop year and this adds to price firmness during October, November, and December. If there is a decline in prices in December, it is the result of the beginning of the Florida harvest. Florida is where about one-fourth of the world's supply of oranges is grown. While demand for orange juice is influenced somewhat by price, the major price determinant is the supply situation. Before taking a position, the trader should consider the main factors affecting the supply of oranges; production, imports, year-end carryover, and cold storage figures. Even when carryover stocks are at record levels, prudent traders will hesitate to establish short positions or bear spreads during the November/February period. The possibility that freezing temperatures could cause fruit damage makes those positions hazardous during the mentioned time frame. It must be noted that temperatures have to remain below 28 degrees Fahrenheit for at least 4-5 hours for significant fruit damage to occur. Cloud cover and wind velocity also must be taken into consideration.

***

LONG SEPTEMBER VS. SHORT JANUARY ORANGE JUICE

This is an old crop/new crop spread. This inter-crop bull spread involves buying September and selling January (next year) at the beginning of the current calendar year. If a freeze, or freeze scare does occur, September will gain on the January contract. The spread should be liquidated late February. Unless a hurricane or other weather catastrophe destroys the crop, the September contract will decline prior to its expiration. If a real shortage is unlikely and September trades at an exorbitant premium above the January contract during the spring (inverted market), a bear spread involving the purchase of January (next year) against the sale of September (current year) may offer a rare trading opportunity. This bear spread tends to perform best in mid-summer. Timing the entry is of paramount importance.

Many traders like to spread November against January. For the bull spread (long Nov/short Jan) the appropriate notes above apply. In case of the bear spread (short Nov/long Jan) the spread

76

could be initiated late in August to mid-September and liquidated late October.

***

SUGAR #11

Two-thirds of the world's trade in sugar takes place in sheltered trading areas. The remaining third of the world supply is referred to as "world sugar" and the #11 sugar futures contract is the one written for "world" or "free" sugar.

The crop year begins in October. Seasonally, October and November are usually the weakest months while April/May tend to be the strongest. The seasonality of sugar is a weak price factor when compared with other stronger influences. For example, high interest rates cause steep declines in world sugar prices because high rates discourage the holding of sugar inventories. World sugar prices are denominated in U.S. dollars and, therefore, when the dollar is strong, sugar prices are depressed. Sugar prices are also known to move relative to precious metal prices.

LONG MAY VS. SHORT OCTOBER SUGAR

This bull spread usually reaches its seasonal low between July and September. At that time a fairly reliable move favoring the May contract begins and extends until January. The two contract months are of the same calendar year, thus, in the fall of 1990 one would long May '91 vs. short the October '91 sugar contract. The spread is normally traded between September 15 and January 15.

***

SHORT OCTOBER VS. LONG MARCH SUGAR

Once the above May/Oct bull spread reaches its peak and the trader expects that bearish fundamentals will exert their influence, the Oct/March (next) bear spread may prove profitable if it is established in April/May and liquidated in August.

77

FIBER & FOREST PRODUCTS

COTTON

In the United States, most cotton is planted between March and May, and harvested during October and November. Weather is the big factor in cotton growth; hot and humid is best. The amount of rain also is important; too much or too little will mean a smaller crop.

During the harvest period, selling of the new crop causes price declines from August highs to October/November lows. During December/January a post-harvest rally may be created by heavy mill buying and heavy exports. After this short run up, however, the price declines steadily and reaches seasonal lows for the year during February/March. During planting season the price begins a slow up-trend. After May, the acreage actually declines for a short time. Then, the uncertainty about both the weather and the condition of the planted acreage during the growing season tends to cause a price surge which lasts from June through August.

***

DECEMBER VS. MARCH COTTON

If market fundamentals are strongly bullish, cotton bull spreads can be profitable and, in limited risk situations, these spreads will protect the trader against the violent shakeouts that so often happen in the cotton market. To set up a bull spread the trader goes long December cotton (December 1990 contract, for example) and short March cotton (March 1991 contract). He should try to buy December at a 100 to 200 point discount to March. This carrying charge spread can often be placed in May and liquidated late June or early July. Another possibility for long December vs. short March is to place the spread during September or October and liquidate it mid-November. In a strong bull market this spread can invert, with December moving to a 100+ point premium to March.

During an economic slowdown, users are reluctant to finance large inventories at much less than the carrying charge.

If cotton is plentiful, each expiring contract may move toward full carrying charges as it approaches maturity. Therefore, if a long March (1991) and short December (1990) cotton spread can be obtained at less than 50% carry (premium March), this bear spread may offer some limited potential. The spread should be initiated late August-early September (year '90 in our example) and held until the third week in November.

Another possible bear spread would be to enter long March ('91) versus short December ('90) cotton, beginning January ('90) and holding until mid-March for a possible 100-200-point profit.

***

JULY VS. DECEMBER COTTON

This is an old-crop/new-crop spread. July is the last futures contract of the current crop year, while December is the first contract offered after harvest is completed. Needless to say, this inter-crop spread is extremely volatile, as are all spreads that cut across crop years. Long July vs. short December bull spread may be profitable if initiated in October or November and held until the end of January. If export demand is strong, another opportunity is to enter the spread in March and hold it into May.

Between mid-April and the end of June, the July cotton contract often weakens after a bull market move. Just as old crop, July, rises swiftly over new crop, December, in a bull market, when the reaction arrives July plummets relative to December. It is hard to pinpoint the initiation period, but the July contract is expected to weaken considerably from early May through expiration.

***

OCTOBER VS. DECEMBER COTTON

Early summer is the time for a seasonal up-move in cotton. In a bullish market October cotton is expected to gain on December, perhaps as high as several hundreds of points premium. This spread is considered limited risk because both October and December are new crop contracts. October, however, is a swing month. An early crop will depress October, particularly if California and Texas crops are abundant, and October will go to discount relative to December cotton. On the other hand, if the crop is threatened and harvest is late, the October will behave more as an old crop month and the October contract will go to a high premium relative to the December contract. Late spring, thus, and early summer are the times to establish long October versus short December cotton bull spreads. Even though October trades at a premium most of the year, as harvest time approaches, October frequently trades at a discount to December. Therefore, one has to watch the October/December spread chart in cotton for possible topping action, and to establish the long December vs. short October bear spread in the expectation that, before the expiration of October, the spread will go to even money. Or, perhaps October will sell at a discount under December during the month of September.

***

LUMBER

Lumber prices reflect the health of the housing industry. The trend depends on the pace of housing starts which, of course, are influenced by interest rates and the availability of money.

While lumber prices have strong seasonal tendencies, the interest rate factor can either magnify, cancel or reverse the seasonal price moves. If interest rates are high but steady, seasonal factors may still affect prices. However, when the prime rate soars from 15% to 20% and then plummets to 11% within a few months as it did in 1980, a reverse roller coaster movement affects

81

the futures prices of T-bills and bonds. And, along with the changes in these interest rate vehicles go the parallel fluctuations in lumber futures. Thus, in an era of high and volatile interest rates, the lumber futures market is just another way of capitalizing on interest rate fluctuations.

From September to December lumber futures generally rise in anticipation of next year's building prospects. From December to March, inventory accumulations often force prices higher if there is strong demand for the cash products. This up-move is followed by a long down trend from March to September, as demand declines. Peak season for construction is the summer and the trader must watch for a sharp hike in late-summer prices. This summer rally is caused by additional demand from construction companies with inventories of lumber too low to sustain construction levels.

***

LONG SEPTEMBER VS. SHORT NOVEMBER LUMBER

The strongest seasonal relationship in lumber is the summer rally; the demand for lumber is often stronger during late summer than early winter. This bull spread should be initiated in late spring or the summer months. Attempt to enter it when September/November trades close to even money.

If market fundamentals are bullish enough, in a time span of a few weeks September could move several hundred points premium over November. This spread may work even in a very bearish situation: If in June the short term interest rates are high and are expected to rise, and the spread is near its historically wide ground, it may offer a quick profit of a few hundred points. Caveat: lumber spreads are not limited risk spreads and, therefore, carrying charges do not limit adverse moves. Stop-loss protection is a must!

***

SHORT JULY VS. LONG SEPTEMBER LUMBER

This bear spread should be initiated during February or March at approximately even money, plus or minus 50 points. If the normal seasonal pattern holds, a good percentage profit can be realized by late May.

***

SHORT MARCH VS. LONG MAY LUMBER

A bear spread that adheres to the seasonal pattern. Beginning mid-December, May strengthens against March and the bear trend lasts until March expires.

On the July/September and March/May bear spreads: Increases in short-term interest rates would exact heavy pressure on the deferred lumber contracts.

NEW AND UPDATED
MARKET SPREADS AND
TRADING OPPORTUNITIES

** For Explanatory Notes Pertaining To Spread Charts Used In This Section, See Appendix Page147 **

METALS

SPREADING IN METALS FUTURES

In a precious metals bull spread, a trader would sell the nearby month and buy the deferred. In precious metals futures, the difference or spread between two contract months reflects the cost of carrying the commodity between the two delivery months. In metals, carrying costs are largely a function of interest rates, or the cost of borrowing money. The higher the price (per ounce price) of gold or silver, the more money one must borrow to finance the purchase of a given amount of gold or silver, and the larger the interest expense. Thus, the widening spread between nearby and distant months in a bullish precious metals market reflects the increasing cost of carry. If a bullish market materializes, the trader would expect that the profit form his long position would be greater than any loss from his short position, thereby resulting in a net profit.

The trader who expects gold prices to fall might put on a bear spread. This trader would expect the differential between the near and far months to narrow over time. In other words, he would expect gold prices for the deferred months to decrease more than prices for the nearby months, thus closing the gap between the near and far months. The rationale for this expectation is that financing costs incurred to purchase gold will decrease as the price of gold decreases. Thus, a bear spread involves buying the nearby month and selling the deferred.

Note: There is one important difference between gold futures prices and currency futures prices. Like gold, currency futures spreads are determined by the "cost of carry." That is, the difference between, say, March gold prices and June gold prices will be just enough to make it worthwhile to store the gold in a bank. Typically, this cost is the interest cost of the loan that finances ownership of the gold. Similarly, the difference between the price of March sterling and June sterling will also be the cost of carrying sterling for three months, with one important difference. When gold is deposited in a bank it does not earn interest - the pound does. Thus, the spread necessary to store sterling at a profit is less than the spread necessary to store gold by the amount of the dollar value of the sterling yield.

In gold futures terminology, one is said to be "long the spread" if one is short the nearby contract and long the deferred contract. Note that this is the opposite terminology to the one prevailing in T-bond and T-bill futures. The reason for the difference might be that a "long spread" is normally associated with a "bull spread." In a bull market, the deferred contract in gold futures will normally gain in price relative to the nearby contract. Whereas in T-bond futures the nearby contract will normally gain in price relative to the deferred contract.

GOLD AND SILVER SPREADS

Gold prices perform best in an inflationary environment. Spreads in gold (and silver) are governed by the yield on certain short-term investments because precious metals are inexpensively storable in bank vaults. The difference between the price paid and the price received should represent a rate of return comparable to the short-term interest rates (for ex.: Eurodollar rates;

bankers' acceptance rates). Keep in mind that the spread always depends on two factors: the price of gold and the short-term interest rates. If one thought that the price of gold was going to rise, one would "buy the spread" by buying the more deferred delivery and selling the nearby. In contrast, if one were bearish on gold prices, one would sell the distant month and buy the nearby month. Note that these actions are just the opposite of those taken when spreading agricultural commodities.

Often gold spreads are leading indicators for interest rates and for the price of gold itself. The following formula is of great interest for those who trade outright positions:

$$\frac{\text{spread differential}}{\text{nearby price}} = \text{yield}$$

COPPER

The housing and the automobile industries are the largest users of copper. Car manufacturers buy copper during the year's first quarter. The construction people buy during late winter and early spring. The large purchases made by these two users push copper prices up from December through March. Then, as the need declines, the season's lows are reached during October and November.

Copper seasonals are reliable. In normal years the price movements are long, strong and, within limits, predictable. Put on limited risk spreads in mid-winter, liquidate them in early spring and seasonal profits can be realized.

***

LONG MAY VS. SHORT DECEMBER COPPER

Put on the long May vs. short December spread during the last week in December or the first week of January and hold it until mid-March to early April. Or, trade it by aiming at a 200-250 point profit and liquidating the spread if and when the hoped for profit is attained. Sharply increased industrial activity and/or falling interest rates will provide excellent profits, even a premium for the May contract if a true bull market in copper develops.

***

PLATINUM VS. GOLD SPREADS

While platinum participates in all precious metals' rallies, one must still remember it is an industrial metal. As the economy accelerates, therefore, platinum tends to gain on gold. Also, a drop in interest rates favors platinum. It is also true, however, that sustained high interest rates would fail to stimulate heavier industrial activity and stockpiling platinum.

Provided the outlook for the platinum/gold spread is favorable on the basis of expanding industrial activity, the trader may consider two seasonal patterns:

First, platinum often makes substantial gains on gold beginning late March. To take advantage of this move, buy two (2) units of July platinum versus the short sale of one (1) unit of September gold. (Platinum on NY Merc., gold on Chicago Merc.).

Second, platinum tends to gain on gold from mid-October to early January. In this instance the trader would go long two units of April platinum (NY Merc.) versus short one unit of April gold (COMEX). These trades should be initiated as platinum nears support levels relative to gold.

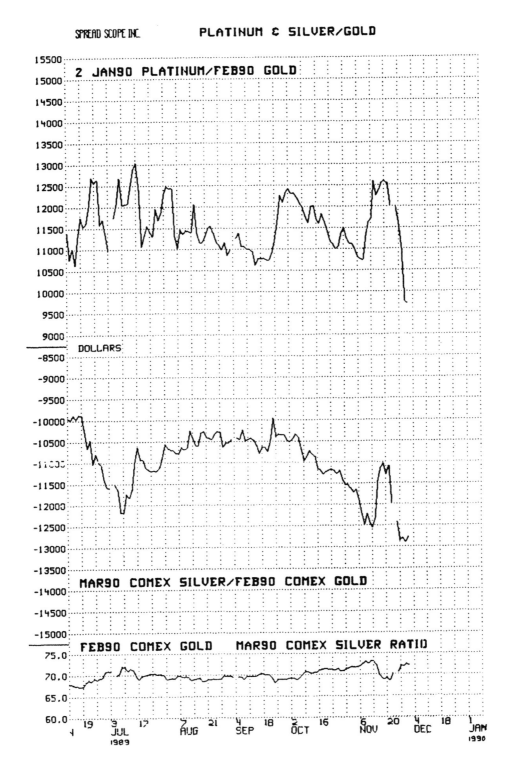

2 JAN90 PLATINUM/FEB90 GOLD

DOLLARS

MAR90 COMEX SILVER/FEB90 COMEX GOLD

FEB90 COMEX GOLD   MAR90 COMEX SILVER RATIO

Chart courtesy of Spread Scope, Inc.

ENERGY COMPLEX

INTRODUCTION

Since the introduction of NYMEX's heating oil contract in 1978, gasoline contract in 1981, and crude oil contract in early 1983, speculators have traded the NYMEX energy complex because of the opportunity to profit from widely fluctuating oil prices.

Oil is the world's largest cash commodity, consequently, over the past decade there have been serious political, social and economic consequences of oil price volatility. Speculative profit potential in futures can be realized only with fluctuating prices in a liquid market, hence the NYMEX energy futures contracts have been particularly good trading vehicles.

ENERGY INTERDELIVERY SPREADS

An interdelivery (intramarket) spread involves the simultaneous purchase/sale of different delivery months of the same commodity.

When adequate energy supplies exist, a carrying charge market should prevail. In that case nearby futures will be priced below the price of distant months by the amount of the carrying cost, which includes interest, storage and insurance.

On the other hand, when supplies are tight, concern over available product often causes prices of the near month to gain relative to the distant months. If there is concern of a shortage, this would result in greater demand for the near-term supplies. Sometimes the near month may go to a premium over the distant months - resulting in an "inverted" market.

Seasonal patterns are important in interdelivery spreads.

Gasoline demand is seasonally low in the winter months but rises in the spring and peaks in June and July as people go on vacation. Memorial Day is the official beginning of the summer driving season. Labor Day is the official end. Because of this seasonal pattern, gasoline stocks reach a peak during February, March and April and hit a trough after Labor Day.

October is the official start of the winter Heating Oil season. From October through March, when demand picks up, distillate stocks are drawn down. At the end of the heating oil season, at the end of March, distillate stocks should be at their lowest level. Demand for heating oil can be seen as a function of temperature: The colder the weather, the higher the demand for heating oil.

INTERDELIVERY SPREAD IN GASOLINE

Example: Gasoline futures for delivery in April traditionally run in the range of 50 to 150 points under Gasoline for delivery in May, during the first quarter of the year.

When the trader notices that April gasoline futures are even or trading over gasoline for May delivery, he wishes to profit from this reversed price relationship between those months. Strictly on the basis of technical analysis, the investor will sell gasoline futures for delivery in April and simultaneously buy the same quantity of gasoline futures for delivery in May. Should the spread between these two months reverse as expected, the trader will buy the April and sell the May gasoline futures at then-current price levels to realize the anticipated profit.

Another example: The trader expects that demand for the coming summer will be lower than normal for gasoline due to improved efficiency of cars, smaller engines and competition from diesel fuel. Normal output by refiners will create a glut in the gasoline market, driving prices down. The trader notes that gasoline for June delivery is trading 80-100 points over gasoline for May delivery. The anticipation is that the May contract will decline less than the June contract in view of the above described market conditions. The trader, therefore, buys gasoline futures for May delivery and simultaneously sells an equivalent quantity of gasoline futures for June delivery. As the spread narrows in response to high output and low demand, the trader liquidates his spread by selling the May futures and buying the June gasoline futures at then-current price levels.

INTERDELIVERY SPREAD IN HEATING OIL

Example: By analyzing June/July heating oil spreads, the trader determines that the spread difference is usually in the range of 5 to 50 points, June over. When the trader notices that June contracts in heating oil futures are trading 125 points over July, he decides to establish a spread in the hope of profiting from this deviation from the normal relationship. He, therefore, sells heating oil futures for delivery in June and at the same time buys the equivalent quantity of heating oil futures for delivery in July. As the price relationship in the spread narrows towards the historically normal range, the trader liquidates the spread by buying the June contract and selling the July heating oil futures contract at the then-current price levels.

Note: For market reading purposes, the trend of the spread is more important than the exact level. The movement of the spread provides a gauge of the supply and demand situation.

July marks the peak U.S. summer driving season, just as February marks the peak heating season. The winter peak occurs in February one year, late December another. The peaks vary. The trader must consider the short-term interest rate, a key term in the cost-of-carry equation. Traders must keep in mind a very important fundamental factor: The energy market will never pay more than full carry, but there is no theoretical limit on an inversion. Traders who guess wrong in a carry-market situation face strictly limited consequences. Traders wrong in a non-carry situation can really suffer.

INTERMARKET SPREAD: HEATING OIL/GASOLINE

Heating Oil vs. Gasoline is an example of a seasonal inter-commodity spread. Gasoline, historically, has been more expensive than other petroleum products because it requires sophisticated processing. While gasoline is usually more expensive than heating oil, during the winter heating oil prices may exceed gasoline prices. Gasoline prices normally increase during the summer driving season and level off in the winter. On the other hand, heating oil prices rise during the winter heating season and level off in the spring and summer.

Example: The investor/trader is aware that the demand for (and thus the price of) heating oil increases as the winter commences and, simultaneously, the demand for and price of gasoline decreases. As winter sets in, the trader wishes to profit from this seasonal activity. Therefore, he buys heating oil futures for delivery in October. Simultaneously, sells an equivalent quantity of gasoline futures for delivery in December.

By spreading these products, the trader establishes an inter-market spread between these two products. The spread will yield a profit should the spread between them narrow. As the spread does narrow, selling the heating oil and buying the gasoline futures, the trader is able to profit from the anticipated seasonal price behavior in these markets.

A SOURCE-PRODUCT SPREAD

This is a type of intercommodity spread between the raw material and its refined product. The so-called "netback," quoted in dollars per barrel, calculates the value of crude oil according to the value of the refined barrel. If a refiner's netback is greater than the market value of crude oil, and he wants to prevent the profit margin from dwindling, he would "put on the crack."

The crack spread indicates buying crude oil futures while simultaneously selling heating oil and gasoline futures. If a trader expected the refiner's processing margin to widen, he would put on a "reverse crack," - buy heating oil and gasoline futures and sell crude oil futures. The trader would buy five heating oil and five gasoline futures while selling ten crude oil contracts.

The "crack spread" can be a valuable market reading tool. The traditional 3-2-1 spread tells refiners how profitable it is to convert three contracts worth of crude oil into two contracts of gasoline and one heating oil. If brokers quote the spread as "310 at 12" it means that you can sell the spread at $3.10 a barrel or buy it at $3.12.

Example: A trader who follows the oil market comes to the conclusion that the current value of crude oil in relation to the current sales value for refined products is weak, giving refiners an unusually large profit margin. The trader anticipates that prices will weaken as a result of slack demand during the third quarter, while crude oil prices will fall by a smaller amount. As a result, the spread between crude oil and products should narrow.

In view of the above, the trader buys crude oil futures in a nearby delivery month. Simultaneously, he will sell heating oil and gasoline futures in deferred trading months which parallel a refiner's production schedule. As the spread between the crude oil and the product futures narrows, the trader sells the crude oil futures and buys the product futures back at the then-current price levels.

THE NYMEX CRACK SPREAD

When crude oil futures were introduced in 1983, they revolutionized the trading strategies of market participants . . . Since the oil industry now could hedge both its raw material input and finished product output prices, the commercial hedgers began spread-trading the industry's profit margin.

Crude oil, gasoline and heating oil prices have moved quite independently of one another. This has exposed the oil industry to significant risks; the risk of rising crude prices, the risk of falling refined product prices, and the risk of a reduction in profit margins. Oil spreads trading provides a mechanism to reduce the risks inherent in generating positive oil industry profit margins. Accordingly, they represent one of today's major financial management opportunities available to the industry.

To the hedger, oil spreads trading serves as a tool to protect the profit margins, or operating income derived from the manufacturing process, i.e., refining. To the trader, oil spreads trading represents a major investment opportunity. The trader attempts to profit by exploiting price fluctuations between crude oil and refined petroleum products. He willingly assumes risk by trying to predict oil spreads movements before they occur and thereby profits from the market's volatility.

NYMEX institutionalized oil spreads by providing a single transaction, simultaneous purchase and sale of all energy contracts traded at the Exchange. It has been termed the NYMEX Crack Spread. By standardizing the Crack Spread, NYMEX has made it easier for all market participants to trade crude to refined product price differentials. The trader may incur less risk when trading Crack Spreads than when trading individual energy futures contracts. However, the margin required for trading Crack Spreads is substantially less than the already low margin requirement for outright position trading. Therefore, the trader's leverage in the Crack Spread is among the highest available in any financial market. Important to note that any combination of crude with either (or both) refined product contracts may comprise a Crack Spread.

Fundamental news on the energy market is available widely. The continual analysis of the oil market simplifies trading the Crack Spread based on fundamental long-term supply and demand considerations. Crack Spread trading in the short run is also possible by analyzing the makeup of each energy market. Then the trader can either identify short-term anomalies among market relationships, or predict the timing of individual energy futures market reactions to internal or external considerations.

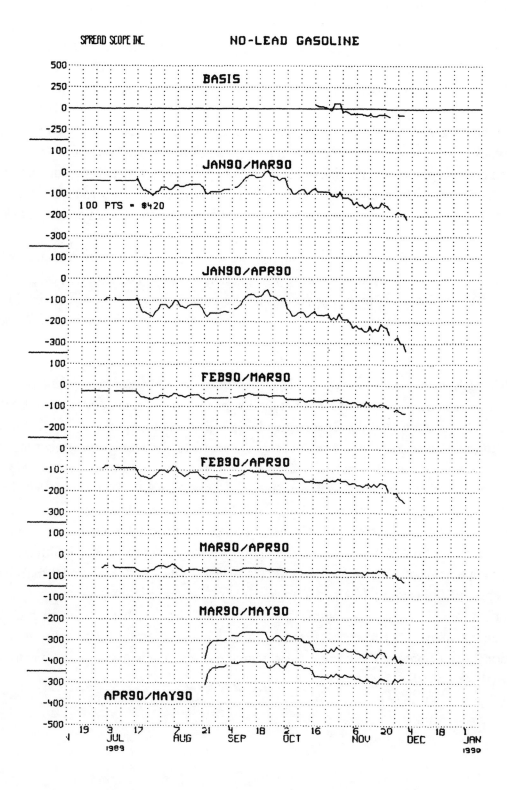

Chart courtesy of Spread Scope, Inc.

96

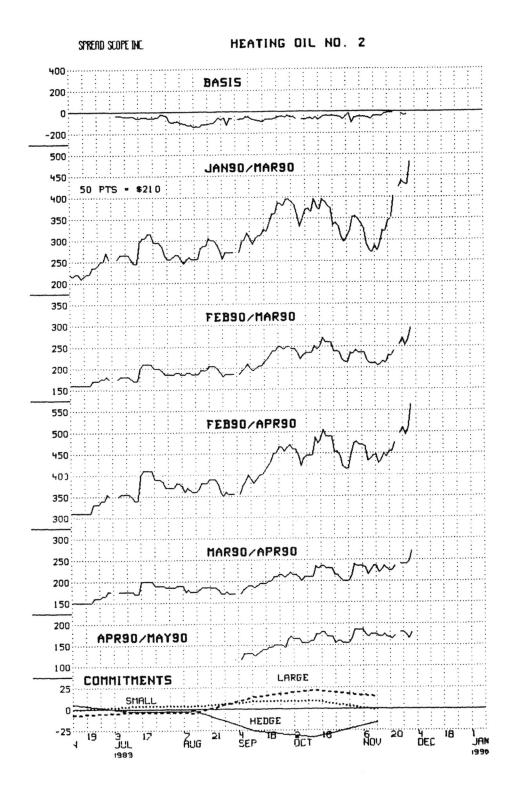

Chart courtesy of Spread Scope, Inc.

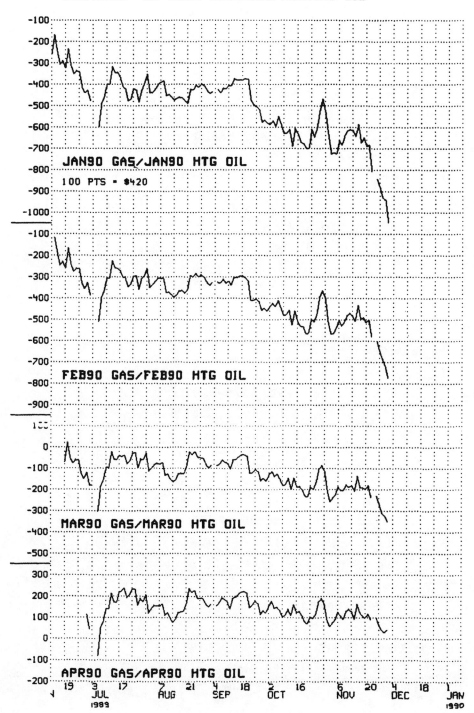

SPREAD SCOPE INC. NO-LEAD GASOLINE/HEATING OIL

JAN90 GAS/JAN90 HTG OIL

100 PTS = $420

FEB90 GAS/FEB90 HTG OIL

MAR90 GAS/MAR90 HTG OIL

APR90 GAS/APR90 HTG OIL

Chart courtesy of Spread Scope, Inc.

98

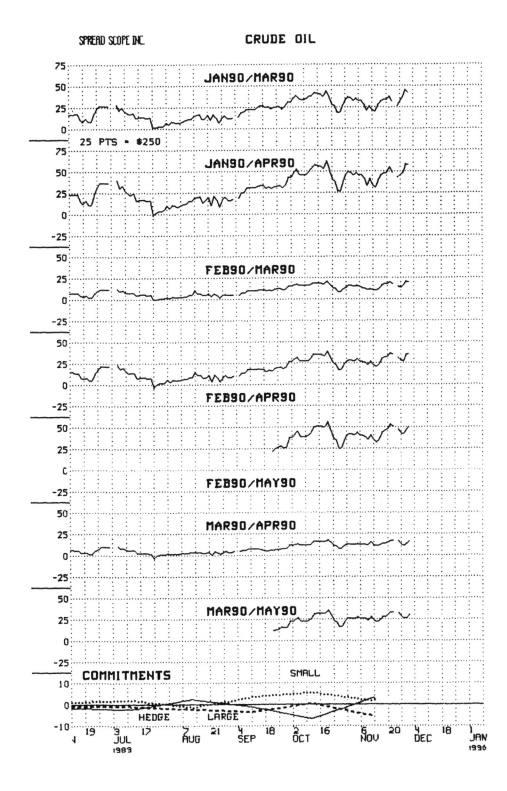

Chart courtesy of Spread Scope, Inc.

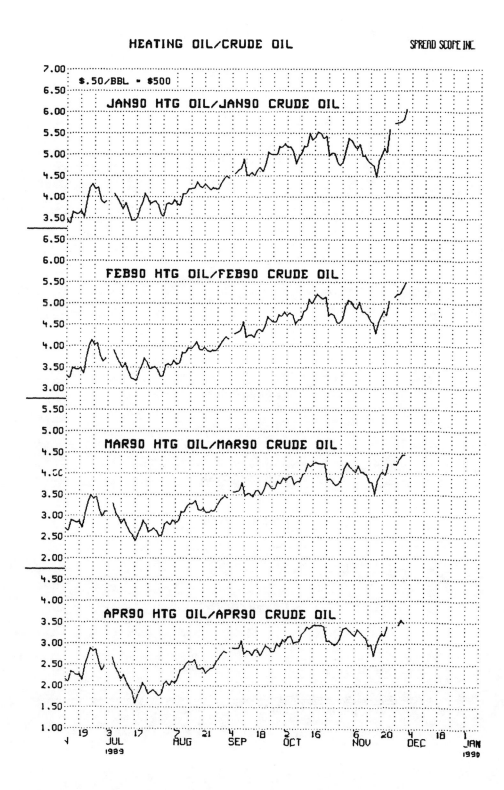

Chart courtesy of Spread Scope, Inc.

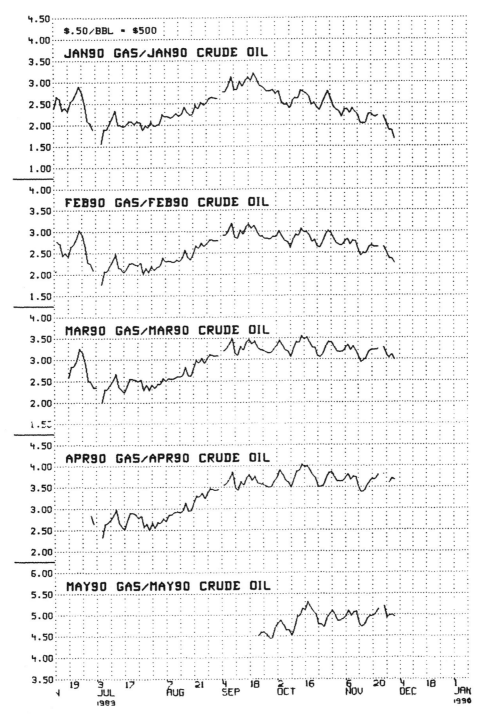

Chart courtesy of Spread Scope, Inc.

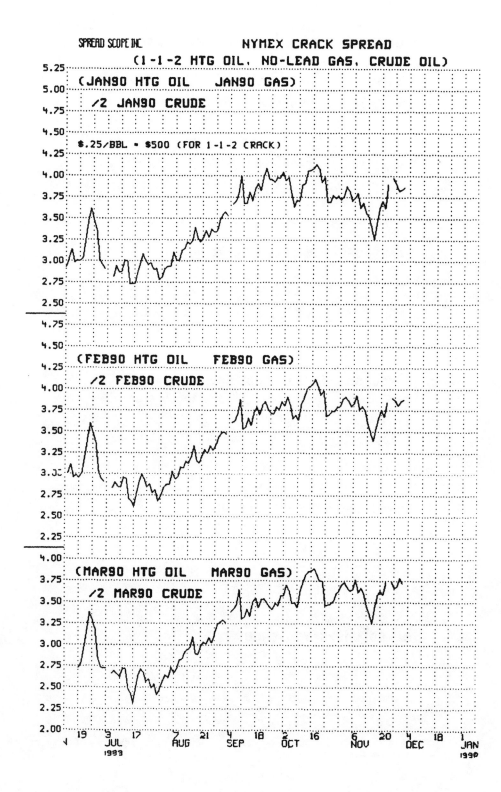

SPREAD SCOPE INC   NYMEX CRACK SPREAD
                (1-1-2 HTG OIL, NO-LEAD GAS, CRUDE OIL)

(JAN90 HTG OIL   JAN90 GAS)

/2 JAN90 CRUDE

$.25/BBL = $500 (FOR 1-1-2 CRACK)

(FEB90 HTG OIL   FEB90 GAS)

/2 FEB90 CRUDE

(MAR90 HTG OIL   MAR90 GAS)

/2 MAR90 CRUDE

Chart courtesy of Spread Scope, Inc.

102

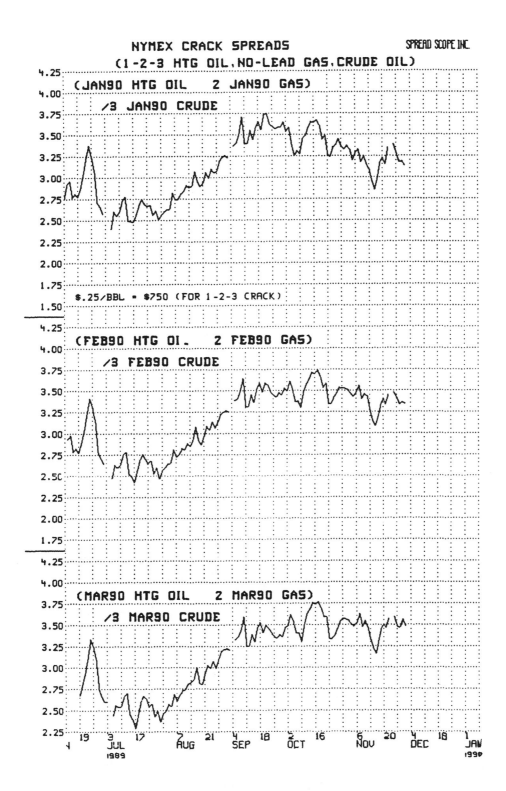

NYMEX CRACK SPREADS
(1-2-3 HTG OIL, NO-LEAD GAS, CRUDE OIL)

SPREAD SCOPE INC.

(JAN90 HTG OIL   2 JAN90 GAS)

/3 JAN90 CRUDE

$.25/BBL = $750 (FOR 1-2-3 CRACK)

(FEB90 HTG OIL   2 FEB90 GAS)

/3 FEB90 CRUDE

(MAR90 HTG OIL   2 MAR90 GAS)

/3 MAR90 CRUDE

Chart courtesy of Spread Scope, Inc.

103

CURRENCIES

INTRODUCTION

Currency futures trading is a big volume business. While the dollar is strong, many speculators are sitting at the sidelines waiting for the strength of the dollar to break. When signs show that the dollar is weakening these speculators will go long in some foreign currency. Then volume in currency futures will really boom.

Speculators are looking at the U.S. dollar versus four major currencies: British pound, Swiss franc, German mark and the Japanese yen. The pound is no longer the reserve currency it formerly was. The yen is quite a bit controlled by the government. The West German Deutsche mark (D-mark) is the most actively traded currency against the dollar in the cash market and, therefore, it is considered the most valid yardstick against which the speculator can measure the value of the dollar. Another reason why traders consider the D-mark as the "key" currency in international foreign exchange markets is the D-mark's role as the surrogate European currency to which other currencies are linked.

Currency futures trade on the 24-hour banking network, called the "interbank" currency market. Hundreds of banks participate worldwide and dozens of them trade in $5 million per minimum transaction.

If you are going to trade currencies, try to obtain the following information about each country:
Level of international monetary reserves
Balance of trade data
Consumer price index
Wholesale price index
Industrial production index
Unemployment
Money supply
Import/export volume index
General economic indicators

By custom, all world currencies are traded and quoted against the U.S. dollar. If one sells a Deutsche mark futures contract, the seller is bullish on the dollar. Conversely, the buyer of a Deutsche mark futures contract is bearish on the dollar.

If one sells a contract of Deutsche mark futures and buys a yen futures contract, the dollar is basically excluded. This is called taking a position on a cross rate basis (long one currency futures, short another), rather than simply an outright position against the dollar. While the dollar is basically excluded, the mark/yen contract size differences yield different dollar amounts, thus creating some dollar risk.

Most world currencies are traded spot (cash) for delivery in two business days. The difference between the spot price (cash) for a specific currency and the currency futures price is a certain number of "points" based on interest rate differentials.

KEY INTEREST RATES

Everything has a price. Money is no exception. Its price, the interest rate, is determined in the marketplace where money is borrowed and lent. Some of the underlying factors that contribute to general economic activity also directly influence the movement of interest rates. These activities, in turn, affect cash and future prices.

Some of these factors are:

1. Balance of payments
2. Inflation and inflationary expectations
3. Fiscal policy
4. Monetary policy
5. Money supply
6. Political developments/uncertainties

These same factors also influence precious metals, foreign exchange and financial futures spreads.

For foreign exchange purposes, the most important interest rates are the EURO-CURRENCY rates. For illustrative purposes we will use the EURO-DOLLAR, which represents about 80% of the market. But the same principles apply to Euro-marks, Euro-francs, etc. Euro-dollars are dollar denominated deposits held outside the USA. If, for instance, you transfer dollars from a US bank to its branch in London, you have created Euro-dollars.

Foreign exchange traders watch Euro-currency interest rates closely. Higher interest rates make a currency both more attractive to hold and more costly to borrow. Due to the quantity, volatility, and visibility of Euro-dollar rates, it has been customary to trade foreign exchange based on changes in US rates.

The FEDERAL FUNDS rate, a key short term rate, is used by "day traders" as a guideline for currency trading. A federal funds' transaction usually involves the purchase or sale of member bank deposits at Federal Reserve Banks for one business day at a specified rate of interest. Because the Federal funds' rate is an indicator of the supply and demand for excess bank reserves, it suggests potential direction for other interest rates. The trader must keep in mind that European markets close between 10:30 and Noon EST, the time frame when European traders adjust their positions. This fact is important for day traders, especially on Fridays. Between 11:30 and Noon EST the Federal Reserve bears watching because the Fed may enter the market to drain or add reserves, and the interest rate markets, naturally, react accordingly.

PRIME RATE changes indicate past rather than future market conditions. Some market participants look to a trend change in the prime rate as positive proof of a major turnaround in interest rates.

CERTIFICATES OF DEPOSIT: (CDs) are important because they are comparable to Euro-dollar deposit rates. CD rate changes can precede Euro-dollar changes.

TIME DEPOSITS are a popular method of raising funds, particularly in Europe.

DISCOUNT AND LOMBARD RATES: changes in these rates generally indicate monetary policy significance. Discount rate changes are important factors influencing the market.

TREASURY BILLS: T-bills are an obligation of government to pay the bearer a fixed sum after a specified number of days from the date of issue. They are sold at a discount through competitive bidding. A large amount of world reserve assets are held in the form of T-bills. One of the greatest forces in foreign exchange is the shifting of reserve assets from one country to another. Reserve asset funds can be very large. Therefore, T-bill rates are very carefully monitored for major yield changes. T-bill prices move inversely to yield. This is not an absolute rule but many traders use T-bills as a barometer for interest rates in general. T-bills, gold and currencies are all traded on the same exchange (the Chicago Mercantile Exchange) which makes it easy for those trading in spreads.

INFLATION RATE is another factor which plays a key role in exchange rate determination. Some experts believe that an inflation rate differential between two countries must be offset by an interest rate differential of the same magnitude.

MONETARY POLICY is another key determinant of exchange rates. Commodity traders usually watch broad money measures, such as the M2 or M3 money supply figures, on a monthly basis. Demand for money is not easily measured. It must be assessed on a per-country basis.

Other INFLATIONARY SOURCES are government budgets, productivity, supply and demand for commodities and labor, and government regulations and tax policies.

The POLITICAL ROLE OF CENTRAL BANKS is well known. Central banks can "manage" exchange rates by several methods. The first, "intervention," is to directly affect exchange rates. Intervention alters supply and demand but it is only a stop-gap measure. Second, a central bank will raise or lower interest rates to affect the exchange rate in a desired way. The third approach is foreign exchange controls. Foreign exchange controls are rather ineffective due to the dynamic forces that determine rates of exchange. Therefore, most central banks prefer the flexibility of floating foreign exchange rates.

Other political factors such as a grain embargo, the freezing of foreign assets, import and export quotas or tariffs and many other factors may enter the picture and must be examined case-by-case.

CURRENCY CHART PATTERNS

Several factors distinguish currency chart patterns from other commodities;
1) Major chart formations take shape over longer periods of time and thus the interpreter gets a clearer picture as to trends;
2) Bull and bear trends last several months or even years and this makes them simpler to distinguish and to follow;
3) Currency patterns in general seem to adhere to accepted chart formation theories;
4) In view of the above, currencies are among the best markets in responding to chart patterns ("Technical approach").

INTERNATIONAL SHORT RATES

%

14.0

12.0

10.0

8.0

6.0

Euro-£

Euro $

Euro DM

Euro Yen

Jne   Jly   Aug   Sep   Oct   Nov
                              (1989)

U.S. SHORT RATES

%

9.0

8.0

7.0

Federal Funds

1-Month
Commercial Paper

3-Month
Treasury Bills

Jne   Jly   Aug   Sep   Oct   Nov
                              (1989)

INTERNATIONAL LONG RATES

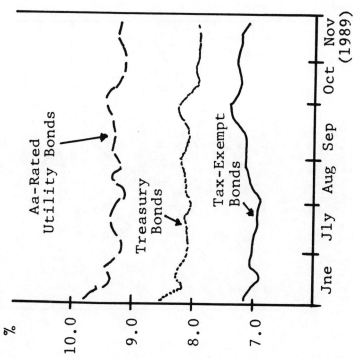

U.S. LONG RATES

110

Fundamentals in currencies, just like any other commodity, also require an analysis of the supply and demand factors. The currency is weak when in oversupply and strong when in overdemand.

There are three major fundamentals which determine the relative price of a given currency versus another currency:

(a) balance of payments;

(b) inflation levels;

(c) interest rates.

INTERDELIVERY CURRENCY SPREADS

An interdelivery currency spread is defined as being long one futures maturity versus short another futures maturity in the same currency. When the trader's expectation is for a shift to a greater interest rate, he would buy the deferred contract and sell the nearby. If a decrease in the interest rate was anticipated, he would establish a long nearby versus short deferred futures position. The purpose of an interdelivery currency spread is to have the price difference (spread) between the two contract maturities either widen or narrow in accord with the intent of the established position. The positions would be liquidated at a profit if the interest rate shifts as per the trader's expectations. For example, if three-month interest rates in Japan are 7% and in the U.S. are at 12%, then the forward discount rate on U.S. dollars is expected to be about 5%. The difference between the March Japanese yen futures and the June Japanese yen futures reflects expectations about what this three-month interest rate differential between the U.S. and Japan will be in March

***

TRADING STRATEGIES: Some guidelines to follow when trading interdelivery currency futures:

• Buy the nearby futures and sell the deferred futures, if:

(a) You expect interest rate differentials to decline when the forward prices are at a premium, or

(b) You expect interest rate differentials to increase when the forward prices are at a discount.

• Buy the deferred futures and sell the nearby futures, if:

(c) You expect interest rate differentials to increase when the forwards are at a premium, or

(d) You expect interest rate differentials to decrease when the forwards are at a discount.

Note 1: Nearbys will gain on deferred in interdelivery currency spreads when there is

111

weakness in the U.S. interest rates, and relative strength in the foreign country's interest rates.

Note 2:   When foreign interest rates are higher than the U.S. rates, interdelivery spreads in the foreign currency futures are inverted.

INTERCURRENCY SPREADS

Intercurrency spreads, also known as currency crosses, are the price relationships between foreign currencies - between yen and pounds, or marks and francs, and other combinations. An intercurrency spread is an intercommodity spread in which the trader simultaneously buys one currency future and sells another currency future short; usually the same delivery month for both currencies. Some crosses are well established and heavily traded, such as the Deutsche mark vs. Swiss franc spread.

Intercurrency spreads fluctuate mainly in response to changes in carrying charges. The carrying charge in currency spreads is the difference in interest rates between the two countries involved. A person who wants to carry currencies must first figure his cost of borrowing U.S. dollars to buy the foreign currency and then calculate the interest he will earn when he deposits the foreign currency just purchased. The difference between the two interest rates is the carrying charge which, naturally, can be a positive or a negative value, depending on which country has the higher interest rates.

As has been shown, an intercurrency spread using currency futures is a position involving long one currency (for example, Dec. SF) versus short another (Dec. DM). Usually the trader will use the same contract maturity for each side of the spread.

In spread trading between any combination of Deutsche marks, Swiss francs and British pounds, margin is limited to the margin requirement of the currency requiring the higher margin for an open position. For the Swiss franc vs. Deutsche mark cross, the initial margin is often less than the margin on francs. On the other hand, crosses involving either the Japanese yen or Canadian dollar require margins for two outright positions. Check with your broker as to margin requirements.

HOW TO SPREAD-TRADE THE BREAK IN THE DOLLAR

There are several potentially profitable ways to earn high returns from a collapsing dollar . . .

A) Buy the Swiss franc and sell the D-mark on a spread.
B) Buy the British pound and sell the Japanese yen on a spread. Caveat: Do this trade only if the break in the dollar is caused by inflation, and oil prices are heading higher.
C) Buy silver and sell gold on a spread. Silver is expected to outperform gold in a bull move

because it responds to industrial use and also to inflation. In a sideways and/or bottoming market this spread may work in the trader's favor since in sideways markets silver is a bit firmer than gold.

D) Buy platinum and sell gold on a spread. Platinum trades 50-oz. contracts. Therefore, buy two contracts for each gold contract sold. The trend must be up in metals. The spread shows seasonal weakness from the end of March until the beginning of April. This is the time to initiate the spread . . . especially when the price of platinum is under the price of gold, and liquidate the spread at a substantial premium.

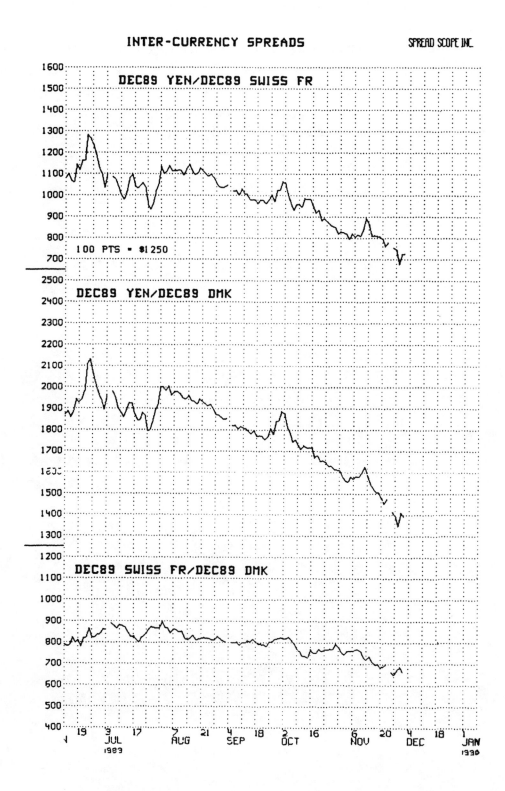

Chart courtesy of Spread Scope, Inc.

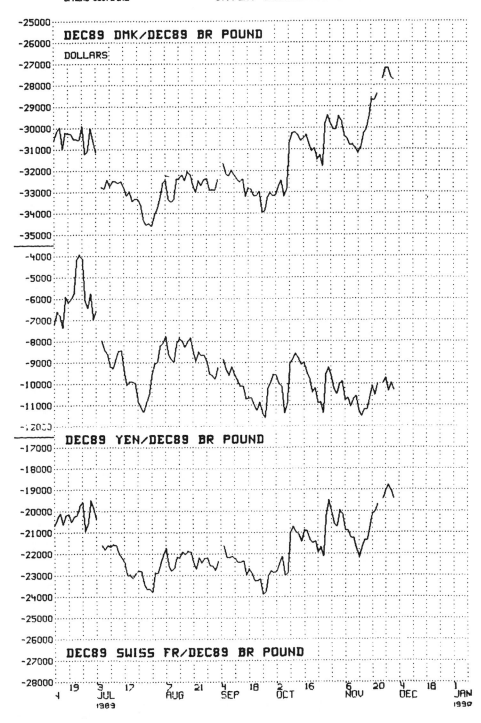

Chart courtesy of Spread Scope, Inc.

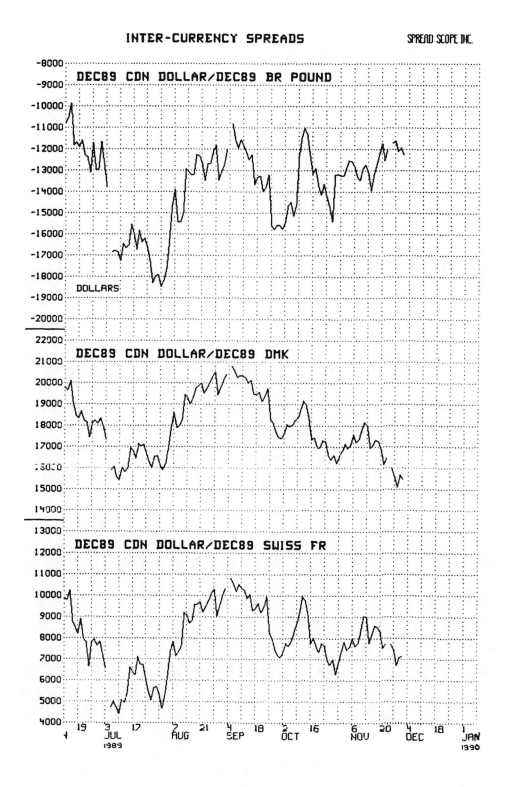

DEC89 CDN DOLLAR/DEC89 BR POUND

DEC89 CDN DOLLAR/DEC89 DMK

DEC89 CDN DOLLAR/DEC89 SWISS FR

Chart courtesy of Spread Scope, Inc.

INTEREST RATE INSTRUMENTS

INTRODUCTION

The introduction of financial futures contracts over the past fifteen years have radically changed the face of the futures industry. As of this writing, Treasury bonds (on CBT) have the largest trading volume, averaging over a quarter million contracts daily, followed by Eurodollars (on IMM) trading over 200,000 contracts.

In June 1985 the municipal bond index futures were introduced (on CBT) and this allowed those who buy and sell munis to hedge their interest rate risk, the same way that holders of T-bills, T-bonds, T-notes, CDs and Eurodollars have been able to do for years.

The muni-bond market is huge. These index futures were immediately well received by portfolio managers, underwriters, dealers and issuers. All these hedgers naturally attract the speculators who want to take the other side of the hedging operations.

The interest from muni bonds is free from all federal income taxes, thus causing them to sell at a premium to T-bonds which are full faith and credit obligations of the federal government. The spread between these two bonds is volatile. (Each full bond point is worth $1,000. The contracts trade in 1/32nds, each worth $31.25. A 1/32nd move is called a "tick.")

T-BILL AND CD FUTURES

Trading CD futures is rather similar to trading T-bill futures. Both are quoted as an index (100 minus the interest rate) and each point is worth $25. Both react to the same economic events and government reports and policies. For example, as the Federal Reserve Board tightens credit, banks compete for available funds by offering higher rates on their CDs. The government competes for available credit by offering higher T-bill rates. But CDs tend to react more dramatically in a given situation. This greater volatility in CDs stems largely from the greater risk associated with a bank's IOU (a CD) versus the government's IOU (a T-bill). (The Treasury always can print more money to meet its debt.) To compensate for the greater risk of bank default, CD holders demand greater return, or higher rate, then do T-bill holders.

Note (re T-bills): Let us say, the one-year bill rate is 10%. That means the bill would sell at a 10% discount from its face value, or $9,000 per $10,000 bill. At maturity you will receive the full $10,000 which means you will earn $1,000 on an investment of $9,000. Thus, you will actually earn an 11.11% "bond equivalent yield" on a "10%" bill. When T-bill rates shoot up, the spread between T-bills and other money market instruments narrows.

An early indication of which way rates will go is the CD/T-bill spread. Expect rates to soften as the spread narrows and to move higher when the spread starts to widen.

Clearly the strategy is to sell CD futures and buy T-bill futures when interest rates begin to rise (and futures prices to fall). The strategy reverses as interest rates decline. This spread became popular on the International Monetary Market (IMM) because the trading pits for T-bills and CDs are right next to one another.

Interest rate spreads are almost always worth considering. A long T-bill vs. short CD trade would benefit from a default by a financially pressed Third World country. If a default, or threat of default were to occur, a "flight to quality" would no doubt take place. Such an occurrence would drive T-bills out to a substantially larger premium over CDs.

Traders should note that CD futures would rise much faster than T-bill futures as interest rates fell. In the past the spread between those markets has widened when there were concerns that banks would have problems meeting CD obligations. This kind of credit risk would diminish as interest rates fall. Thus, the spread between CD and T-bill futures would narrow. Note that most discount brokers would require that you pay commissions on both the bills and the CDs.

THE CD/T-BOND SPREAD

Long-term interest rates are less volatile than short-term. A 15-29 year T-bond futures contract covers the long term. A 90-day CD futures contract covers the short term. As we know both long and short term rates have a tendency to move the same way, but at different speeds. This is a very dynamic spread!

THE YIELD CURVE

The relationship between interest rates and the maturities (short-term to long-term) of debt instruments with the same rating can be graphed in a so-called "yield curve." In US financial markets, the yield curve is based on US government debt instruments. The yield curve can assume several different shapes.

(1) The most common shape of the yield curve is a gradual upward slope. In this instance, the yield curve is termed "positive" or "normal" because long term interest rates are higher than short term interest rates. A yield curve that ascends steeply indicates that the markets expect that interest rates and inflation are headed higher. Investors who commit their money for a longer time period are compensated with a higher interest rate.

(2) On the other hand, if short-term interest rates exceed long-term interest rates, then the yield curve slopes generally downward and is referred to as a "negative" or "inverted" yield curve. A negative yield curve can occur during a period of pronounced inflation, as happened in early 1981 when heavy demand for credit forced short-term rates well above the levels of long-term rates.

(3) The yield curve flattens out when short-term yields are only slightly below long-term rates. This is a transitional state that can occur either when rates have bottomed out and are heading higher, or when rates are coming down. Therefore, the shape of the curve itself does not tell us what to do unless we follow how it is changing.

To sum up: What the yield curve shows is whether monetary policy is tight or loose. Easy money tilts the yield curve steeply upward; tight money inverts it. The yield curve is the financial markets view of money . . . easy or tight.

Debt instruments with maturities of less than a year are known as "bills," those with maturities from one to 10 years are known as "notes," and those with maturities ranging from 10 to 30 years are called "bonds."

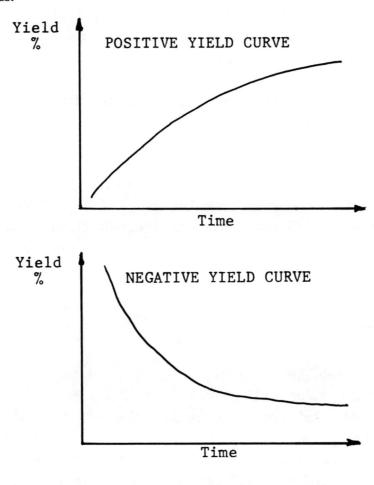

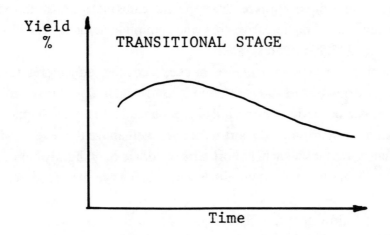

YIELD CURVES

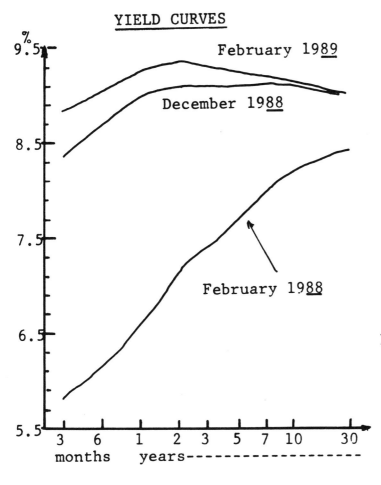

February 1989

December 1988

February 1988

months   years- - - - - - - - - -

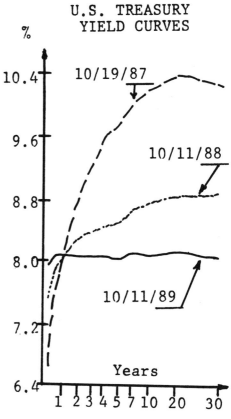

U.S. TREASURY YIELD CURVES

10/19/87

10/11/88

10/11/89

Years

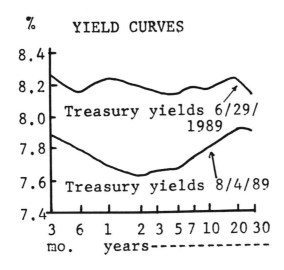

YIELD CURVES

Treasury yields 6/29/1989

Treasury yields 8/4/89

mo.   years- - - - - - - - -

INVERSION OF YIELD CURVE

In early 1989, short-term interest rates rose above longer-term rates, creating what is termed an inverted yield curve. Inverted yield curves often precede recessions by several months. The 1982 economic downturn was preceded by a yield curve inversion 16 months before, in 1980. Since 1953, there have been seven U.S. economic recessions, five of them preceded by an inverted Treasury yield curve. The changes in the spread between the 10-year Treasury rate and the one-year Treasury rate show this relationship. This spread reflects the slope of the yield curve between these two maturities. When the spread is negative, the yield curve is inverted.

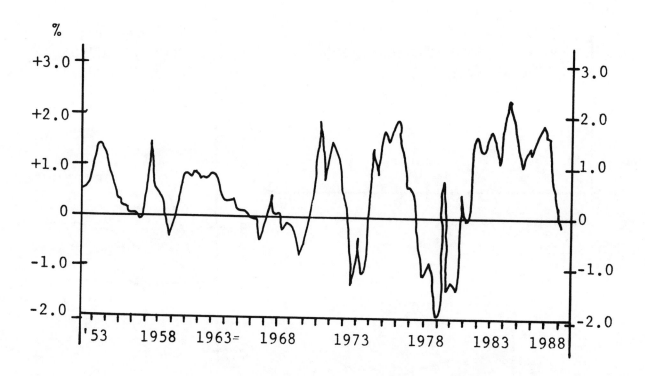

Spread between 10-year and one year Treasury rates.

SPREAD TRADING IN INFLATIONARY AND RECESSIONARY MARKETS

The relationship between interest rates and inflation is of prime importance. Inflation means that the buying power of the dollar decreases. Bond markets usually attempt to compensate for the loss of buying power by raising the interest rates to levels high enough to offset the rate of inflation expected for the period of the loan. When the interest rate markets function in this manner, interest rates tend to increase as the pace of inflation increases. Lenders tend to respond to inflation by pegging interest rates above the rate of inflation. If inflation was increasing at, say an annual rate of 10%, lenders might charge 14% for intermediate term loans. The 14% would include 10% compensation for the anticipated rate of inflation. The remaining 4% represents the "real" rate of interest as opposed to the "nominal" 14% rate of interest which includes the 10% inflation factor.

The effect of the above described process on commodity prices is complex. Basically, it is a kind of battle for profits between the lenders and borrowers. Commodity buyers are usually in the borrowers' category because they frequently borrow money to finance their market transactions. As long as inflationary increases in commodity prices provide adequately large net profits, borrowers will be willing to disregard interest rates.

However, this process of commodity prices and interest rates racing upward together is not endless. The inflation/deflation cycle runs its course. At some point, interest rates fully anticipate and even perhaps over-anticipate the rate of inflation. When this occurs, and the "real" interest becomes relatively high, the acquisition and carrying of commodity inventories by the "trade" is discouraged and the profit potential for the trader/investor may be virtually eliminated. In this way, interest rates, of necessity, increase during inflationary periods until the high interest brings about an economic correction.

Recessions: In general, interest rates begin to decline in the first half of a recession . . . sometimes at a very early point in time in apparent anticipation of the recession. They then tend to remain low for some time after they have bottomed. That is, they rarely spring back up but rather move upward slowly in the ensuing recovery period.

When a recession is beginning, the higher interest rates can (temporarily) work in tandem with reductions in corporate and individual disposable income to decrease demand for commodities. Corporate (and personal) borrowing often increases in early stages of a recession, reflecting the financing of inventories while sales slacken and the efforts to obtain funds in lieu of sales revenues. But such borrowing cannot continue to compensate for diminished revenues. Once such borrowing decreases, it helps interest rates to decline. The subsequent (relative) depletion of inventories allows for subsequent recoveries. (A recession is, by definition, two or more consecutive quarterly declines in the Gross National Product; thus, it is a convergence of many economic trends.)

Interest rate futures price movements appear to be the most consistent in their response to the business cycle. They move inversely. During periods of recession, financial futures prices will advance; the steeper the recession, the sharper the advance. The reason is quite simple: During recessions the demand for money is reduced. Interest rates are really nothing more than the price of money. The interest rate peak tends to occur at the turning point from boom to recession. However, this strength is short-lived and as the recession takes hold, belt-tightening is implemented all along the lines of production. Inventories are cut back, employment is reduced and financial and capital expansion plans are postponed. Short-term interest rates fall very rapidly in the initial stages of a recession. Longer term rates decline more modestly, but more persistently. Short-term rates tend to recover earlier than do the longer term rates (long term government bonds and mortgage rates.) It is important to note that financial futures also will be affected by the direct actions of the Federal Reserve and the Government.

NOTE: Interest rates show not only the return you can get on your investments but also the mood of the market. When rates are high, the market sees economic problems; when they go down, investors are more confident.

The spread between rates can also be informative - sometimes more than the rates themselves. (Example: If the spread between the 3-month T-bills and 30-year Treasury bonds is about 2%, the yield curve is essentially flat, providing barely more return at the long end than at the short end. This means that the market appears to be looking toward a sustainable recovery and a lower inflation rate.)

INTEREST RATES - INFLATION AND MARKET TRENDS

————————F U T U R E S————————

Variables		Precious Metals	Currency	Interest Rates	Energy	Stock Index
Interest rates:	Low	Strong	Strong	Strong	Strong	Strong
	High	Weak	Weak	Weak	Weak	Weak
Inflation:	Low	Weak	Weak	Strong	Weak	Strong
	High	Strong	Strong	Weak	Strong	Weak
Stock Market:	Weak	Weak	Weak	Weak	Strong	Weak
	Strong	Strong	Strong	Strong	Weak	Strong
Energy Prices:	Low	Weak	Strong	Strong	Weak	Strong
	High	Strong	Weak	Weak	Strong	Weak
Dollar:	Weak	Strong	Strong	Strong	Strong	Strong
	Strong	Weak	Weak	Weak	Weak	Weak

THE M.O.B. SPREAD

One of the popular spreads is called the "MOB" spread. The acronym stands for "municipals over bonds."

If you look at the prices of T-bonds and municipal bond contracts, you will see that the difference (the spread) in their prices narrows as expiration approaches. Traders who buy long the muni bond contract, and sell short the T-bond contract expiring in the same month, believe that the narrowing will continue because they expect increased tax rates. If they are correct, then tax-free municipal bonds will be in increased demand and thus will gain on the T-bonds. This strategy is called "buying the MOB spread." If you "sell the MOB," you are long T-bond futures and short muni futures.

Technical factors are vital when deciding whether to buy or sell the MOB. Basically, you "buy" the spread when it is at the lower end of its trading range, and sell at the high end of the range. Stop-loss points must be set to protect yourself against big losses.

As interest rates fall, the MOB spread narrows. A rise in interest rates will produce an increase in the MOB spread. Investors who trade the MOB should understand that they are trading two very different instruments. Since MOB traders spread an index-based futures contract (e.g., munis) against a non-index based futures contract (e.g. T-bonds), they need to be very knowledgeable about the Index.

To sum up: If an investor/speculator expects the relative yield to rise then he should buy the Municipal contract and sell the Treasury contract (that is, go long the MOB spread). If, however, an investor expects relative yields to fall then he should go short the MOB spread. Remember that changes in relative yields can translate into large changes in the level of the MOB spread.

A simple one-to-one MOB position may be adversely affected by movements in the level of long-term interest rates. The investor could possibly protect the value of his MOB position from movements in the level of long-term interest rates by giving one side of his MOB position more weight then the other. A weighted MOB position means that the number of muni contracts bought (sold) does not equal the number of T-bond contracts sold (bought). The Weighting factor is defined as the number of muni contracts bought (sold) for each T-bond contract sold (bought). The expression, "a weight of two" means that (assuming a long MOB position), the investor is long two muni contracts for each T-bond contract that he is short.

THE N.O.B. - SPREAD (T-NOTES VS. T-BONDS)

A one point change in yield will have more impact on the 30-year bond than on the 10-year note. Bonds tend to be weaker than notes in a bear market; stronger in a bull market.

A trade called the "NOB" (notes-over-bonds), spreads the Chicago Board of Trade's T-note against its T-bond futures.

In a rising yield environment, the strategy is to buy the NOB; that is, buy T-note futures and sell T-bond futures. In a declining yields environment, one simply does the opposite - sell the NOB (sell notes and buy bonds). The simplest NOB trade is a one-to-one spread. The timeliness of this trade is greatest around the quarterly refunding period of the US Treasury: late in November, February, May and August. Traders usually begin buying the NOB about 30 days before and through the refunding period for maximum profit potential.

The NOB spread offers investors the chance to play the changing yield-curve relationships. Two basic yield-curve movements: (1) parallel yield-curve shift when all interest rates rise or fall simultaneously, and (2) when the shape of the curve changes. Normally, the yield curve is upwardly sloped, indicating that long-term yields exceed intermediate and short-term yields. The curve gets steeper if long-term yields advance against shorter term yields. When the long-term premium declines against shorter maturities, the curve flattens. In extreme cases the curve "inverts" because short-term yields are at a premium to long-term yields.

To capitalize on parallel yield-curve shifts, the investor must remember (as we pointed out earlier) that a 1% yield change in a long-term security results in a more volatile price move than a 1% yield change in an intermediate-term security.

The NOB can be used to speculate on yield-curve changes. The rule of thumb is: buy the NOB if the yield-curve is expected to steepen and sell the NOB when the yield-curve is flattening. Also, adjustments in the NOB spread ratio can be made.

This advance technique is known as trading the NOB with a "tail." The trader expects the yield-curve to change, either flattening or steepening. Accordingly, instead of a one-to-one spread, the trader calculates the number of notes to bonds required to neutralize the difference in price changes of notes and bonds. The extra T-note contracts are called the "tail."

THE T.E.D. SPREAD (T-BILLS VS. EURODOLLARS)

Eurodollars are US-dollar denominated deposits in banks situated outside the US. All principal and interest payments are made in dollars, regardless of the country in which the transaction takes place.

Traders in Eurodollars watch three cash-market rates: (1) The overnight Fed funds rate, (2) the overnight Eurodollar rate, and (3) the three-month Eurodollar rate in London: called the LIBOR (London Interbank Offered Rate). LIBOR is used by cash-market traders and it also provides the final settlement price for the Eurodollar futures contract on delivery day.

A number of commodity exchanges offer futures contracts in financial securities, including T-bills, T-bonds, CDs and also Eurodollar time deposits.

There are methods of profiting from future changes in interest rates with a limited downside risk. One of these strategies closely followed by professional arbitragers was first described in their newsletters by Douglas R. Casey and John A. Pugsley. The strategy involves a spread between T-bill futures against Eurodollar futures, known as the TED spread.

Trading in TED spreads takes advantage of the so-called "flight-to-quality" phenomenon. As direct obligations of the US Treasury, T-bills are considered risk free. Eurodollar deposits are not guaranteed by any government. While they are direct obligations of the commercial banks accepting the deposits, the Eurodollars are unauthorized and unregulated. Thus, because they are less risky, T-bills offer a lower rate of interest than Euros. A spread of long T-bills/short Eurodollars has evolved to take advantage of the market's desire for quality.

Both T-bills and Eurodollars are quoted by means of an index equal to 100 minus the annualized discount rate expressed as a percentage (e.g., 88.75 for a discount rate of 11.25%). So it is the index, not the interest rate itself, that is traded. (Note: The index rises when interest rates fall!) The price of a T-bill contract will always be higher than the price of a Euro contract of corresponding maturity.

The trader knows that the difference of T-bills minus Eurodollar prices expands when US interest rates decline and contracts when US interest rates rise. The TED spreader's problem is to answer the question: is the T-bill premium too big or too small?

When the TED spread differential is about 50-100 basis points, it is a low risk and high potential opportunity. If the stop-loss is placed 40 points below the initial spread difference, then the risk is $1,000 per contract (that is, per spread). The upside potential is conservatively 300 points (or, $7,500) and if there develops a financial crisis, the upside potential can be 600 points ($15,000) or more. Theoretically, there is no upside limit, and the spread (long T-bill/short Euros) should widen whether the crisis is accompanied by inflation or deflation! Either way, the Eurodollar market will be in serious trouble.

In other words, the best time to enter this trade is when the spread is 1% or less (long T-bills over short Euros). When the spread is very high (6% or more) and seemingly topping out, the trader hopes to profit when the spread narrows. Therefore, under these circumstances he will go short T-bills and long Eurodollars. This trade is NOT recommended because while in the first instance the risk is limited (when the initial spread is very narrow), in the second situation there is no real upside limit in the size to which the spread might widen.

To enter the spread you would put up the initial margin required by your broker plus extra margin money to cover the spread down to the lowest point you felt the spread may narrow. The extra margin money ought to be put by the broker into a money market account where it would earn current interest rates. In case of margin calls the broker would transfer funds from the interest bearing account into your margin account. The best arrangement is when the broker is willing to accept a Treasury bill for deposit and uses the bill as collateral for the margin.

A SAMPLE T.E.D. SPREAD

To calculate the spread, look in the financial tables of the Wall Street Journal labeled "Interest Rate Instruments" to determine what the TED spreads are for future dates. To get the respective yields, you look for the "yield-settle" figures in the IMM Eurodollar table, and the "discount-settle" figures in the IMM Treasury bills table. If you had taken a look at the January 23, 1990 issue of the WSJ, these are the relevant facts you would have distilled from those tables:

Dates:	Yields		Spreads
March 1990	Eurodollar	8.28%	
	T-bill	7.35%	.93%
June 1990	Eurodollar	8.33%	
	T-bill	7.21%	1.12%
September 1990	Eurodollar	8.40%	
	T-bill	7.22%	1.18%

You decide to go with the Sept. '90 contracts. Remember that you will want to buy your T-bill and Eurodollar contracts in a period of relative calm . . . yet when you see serious financial problems on the horizon. To minimize your risk, you also want to employ the TED spread strategy ONLY when the current spread is historically narrow. This is very important because any narrowing of the spread after you trade causes you to lose money at the rate of $25 per basis point, or $2,500 per percentage point . . . just as any increase in the spread after you trade causes you to gain money at that rate.

Let us assume that a financial crisis erupts between the end of January 1990 and September 1990. As the table below shows, the yield on the T-bill will rise to 8.25% from its present 7.22%. The return on your Eurodollar contract will rise to 11.75% from its present 8.40%. The spread on this trade, therefore, will increase 3.50% (11.75 - 8.25) from its present 1.18%. That is an increase of 2.32 percent, or 232 basis points. Since you gained $25 for each basis points, your profits come to 232 x 25 = $5,800 for this transaction.

	In Jan. '90	On Or Before Sept. '90	Increase/ Decline
Eurodollar Yield	8.40%	11.75%	+ 3.35%
T-bill Yield	7.22%	8.25%	+ 1.03%
TED Spread	1.18%	3.50%	+ 2.32%

(In other words, you gained $8,375 on the Eurodollar and lost $2,575 on the T-bill, so your net profit per spread came to $5,800.)

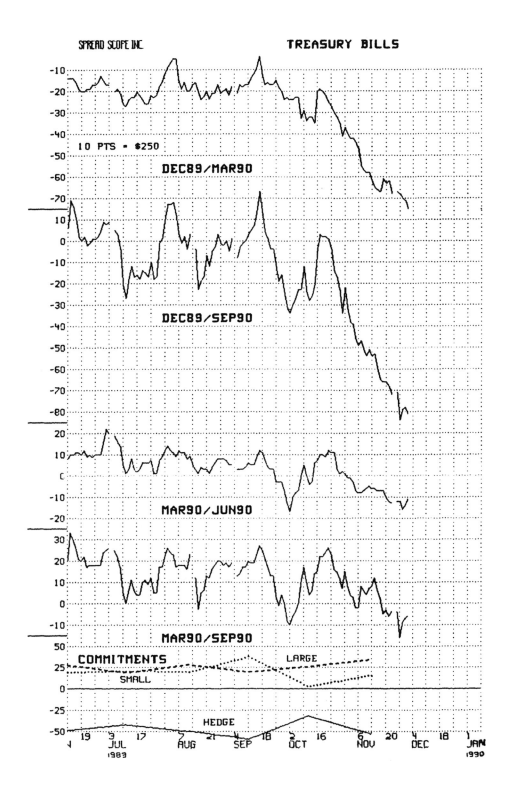

Chart courtesy of Spread Scope, Inc.

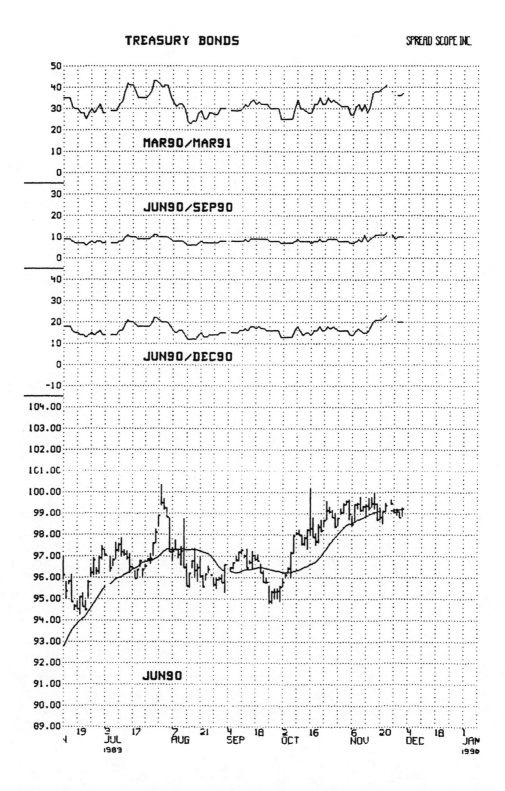

TREASURY BONDS   SPREAD SCOPE INC.

Chart courtesy of Spread Scope, Inc.

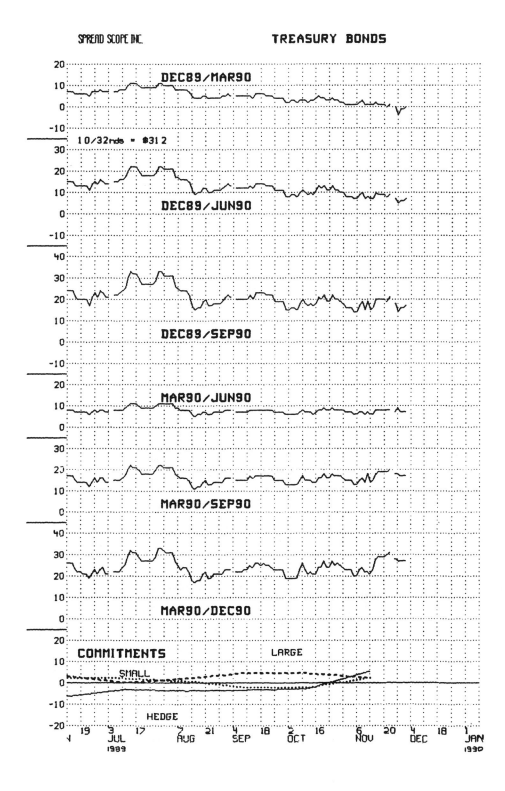

Chart courtesy of Spread Scope, Inc.

131

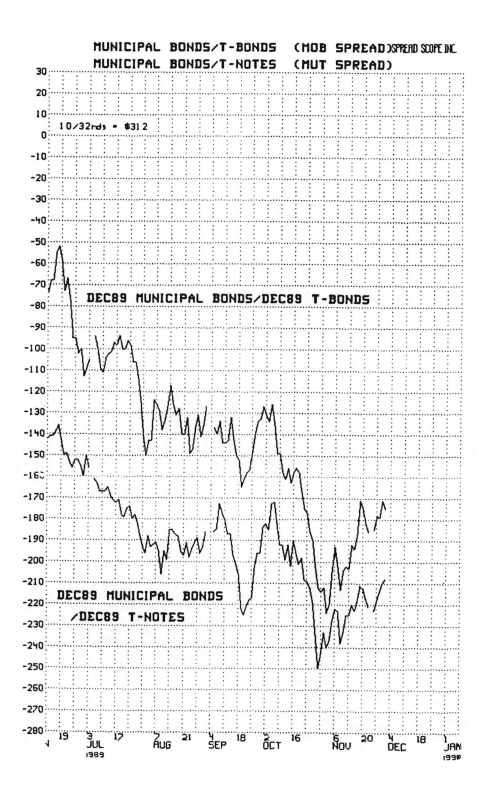

MUNICIPAL BONDS/T-BONDS (MOB SPREAD) SPREAD SCOPE INC.
MUNICIPAL BONDS/T-NOTES (MUT SPREAD)

10/32nds = $312

DEC89 MUNICIPAL BONDS/DEC89 T-BONDS

DEC89 MUNICIPAL BONDS
/DEC89 T-NOTES

Chart courtesy of Spread Scope, Inc.

132

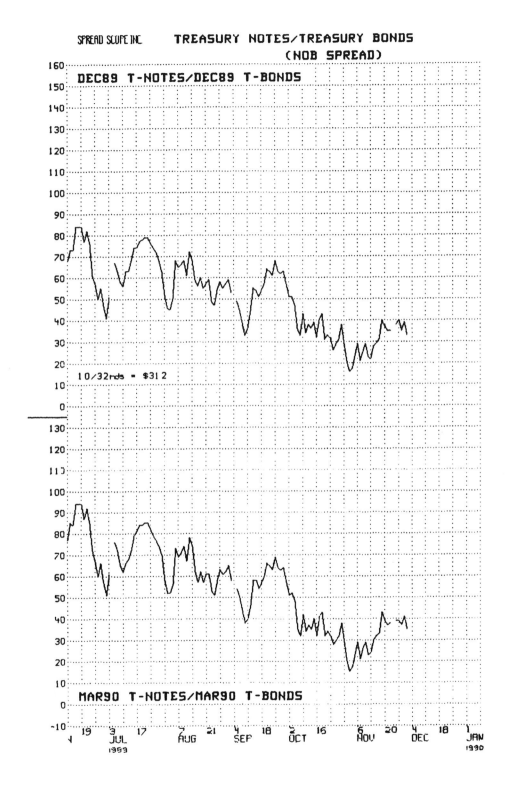

EURODOLLARS

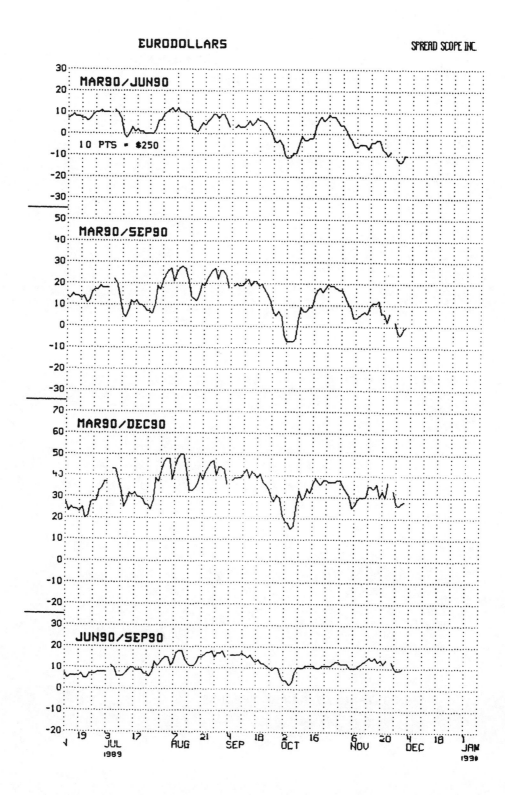

Chart courtesy of Spread Scope, Inc.

134

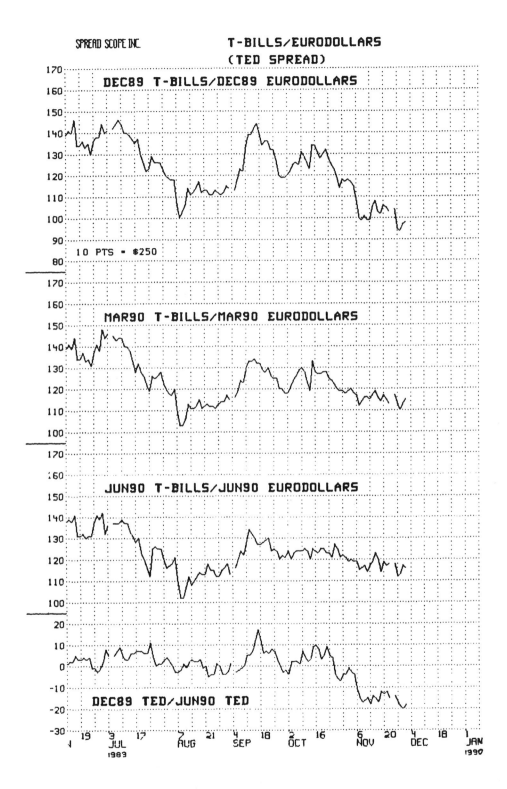

Chart courtesy of Spread Scope, Inc.

STOCK INDICES

STOCK INDEX SPREADS

Some traders spread one stock index contract month against another to profit from the difference in price moves. Such spreads allow traders to speculate on the direction of stock prices with much less risk.

The VALUE LINE COMPOSITE AVERAGE INDEX (traded on the Kansas City Board of Trade) is an equally weighted, geometric average, expressed in index form. It consists of approximately 1,700 stocks, which comprise about 96% of the dollar trading volume in US equity markets. The equal weighting and broad composition of the Value Line Composite Average Index makes it responsive to the so-called second-tier stock price movements.

The STANDARD & POOR'S 500 STOCK INDEX (which trades on the Chicago Mercantile Exchange) is a weighted average. That is, the price of each of the 500 stocks making up the average is multiplied by the number of shares of that issue outstanding. Obviously, large capitalization stocks in this index will have a much bigger effect on the value of the index then will smaller-capitalized issues. Since highly capitalized stocks tend to move sluggishly, the S&P 500s will be less volatile than the Value Line Composite Index. In a bull market, substantial price movements occur, first in the S&P 500 Index, as investors initially buy the large capitalization issues represented heavily in the Index. Then investors turn their attention to the second-tier issues that contribute equally in the Value Line Index. As the bull market develops, these more volatile issues begin to fly. Thus the spread between the Value Line Index and the S&P 500 Index widens.

Just the opposite happens when a market correction begins. First, large investors, mostly institutions, sell the large capitalization issues. So the spread continues to widen, even as a correction gets underway. As the market consolidation continues and investors become concerned about conserving capital, they start to dump their second-tier issues, and the Value Line Index starts to fall faster than the S&P 500s, causing the spread difference between them to narrow.

As we see, the indexes are computed in quite different ways, which causes them to respond differently to a given price change of an individual stock. A few issues can cause wide swings in the value of the S&P 500s, but, to produce that effect in the Value Line Index, a large number of issues have to move in the same direction. In the 1982-83 rally individuals bought the less well capitalized issues, sending the Value Line Composite Index (in July '83) to a 39-point premium over the S&P 500s. The 1985-86 rally was largely fueled by institutional buyers, while individuals either sat it out, or perhaps turned their equity money over to mutual funds. As a result the Value Line Index, in late May, after steadily losing ground all year, dropped to a discount to the S&P 500s. Index trading is not low-risk and it must be closely watched.

The S&P 500 and the NYSE COMPOSITE INDEX contracts differ in size (with the NYSE, incidentally, being traded on the New York Futures Exchange). How many S&P 500s would one spread against the NYSE Composite Index? It is a 7 to 4 spread: One does 7 New Yorks to 4 S&P 500s or 11 New Yorks to 6 S&P 500s, or else 14 to 8.

Signals: There are three main signals traders look for: They watch the cash spreads, they watch the futures spreads, and they watch the spreads between the spreads (which is called the premium).

Calculating Premiums: A = NYSE cash x 7
                                      B = S&P cash x 4
                                      C = NYSE futures x 7
                                      D = S&P futures x 4

                                      A-B = cash spread; C-D = futures spread
                                      Futures spread - cash spread = premium

The 3-month June/September and September/December spreads may offer some interesting arbitrage opportunities. Theoretically, the spread differences between the two 3-month spreads should be identical, if market expectations regarding interest rates and dividend yields are identical for the two periods. Significant spread differences may occur only if the expectations differ significantly for the two periods. If, for example, the June/September spread is larger than the September/December spread by about 25 to 40 basis points, the potential spread trade would be: buy one June/sell two September/buy one December contracts. The reverse spread should be implemented if the September/December spread exceeds the June/September by more than 80 basis points.

If, for another example, the December contract was trading at about 80 basis points over September and the September was trading at about 10 basis point under June (a 90 point difference between the spreads), the potential trade would be to sell June/buy two September/sell December. (This type of spread is called "butterfly" in the commodity trade.) It is rather conservative and the potential profit is generally not very large.

Another, more volatile spread to watch is the June/December six-month spread. Because the time span is doubled, the profit and risk are both larger. The low risk entry point is when the spread is around zero, at which time a sell June/buy December spread might be a profitable strategy.

NOTE: The would-be trader who's attracted to the opportunity for profit in stock index futures but is put off by the high risk, might want to spread-trade index futures. There are two key types of spreads: so-called interdelivery (intramarket) spreads, between contract months of the same index, or the so-called intermarket spreads, between stock index futures traded on different exchanges. Remember, the spread trader attempts to make money on a change in the price differential between two contract months. Basically, spreading involves selling overpriced contracts and buying undervalued contracts, and, hopefully, profiting from the difference.

A simple interdelivery spread could be set up between June and March Value Line Index futures contracts. The trader feels that the June contract is undervalued in terms of the March contract. Expecting a bull market, the trader thinks the distant June contract will rise faster than the nearer March contract. The broker is told specifically to buy the June contract and sell March, and the trader specifies the price differential (not the prices!) he seeks, say, June 75 points over March. After a few weeks time, the price relationship changes, say June gained whereas March has neither gained nor lost. The spread widened and the result: a profit on the spread. In general, contract months tend to move together, although at not the same rate. This is why spreading can be profitable.

Interdelivery spreads are lower in risk than intermarket spreads. Trading intermarket spreads between contract months of different index futures on different exchanges we have to take into consideration the dollar value of the underlying indexes. Therefore, we must balance the two legs of the spreads by buying or selling more contracts of one index and less of another. This ratio, of course, depends on the current trading level. If, let us say, the S&P 500 contract is valued at $60,000 and the New York Stock Exchange Composite Index is valued at $33,000 and the Value Line Index contract is worth $61,000, we will spread two New York Composite for every single contract of S&P 500 or Value Line. Traders usually spread the same contract month in both markets. It is also important to spread only liquid months (an illiquid contract has small open interest). Finally, unless there is a reason why one or more contract months are "out-of-line," do not tie up money in spread positions.

NOTE: Spreaders who are optimistic about the market would arrange what is known as a BULL SPREAD. When the stock market is in an uptrend, prices on contracts in more deferred settlement months are apt to rise faster than nearby month contract prices. So a "bull spread" involves selling a nearby contract month short and buying a distant month contract. If, as the spreader anticipated, the stock market climbed and the spread between the more distant December contract and the nearby June contract widened (as an example), this produced a net spread profit.

Bull spread example: Sell June index and buy December index future at a spread differential of 2.50. Eventually close out the position by buying June and selling December index future contracts at a spread differential of 2.25. The change in spread value is .25. The spread between the more distant contract and the nearby contract widened, producing a spread profit (.25 x $500 = $125. Warning: In certain other futures markets (e.g. - Treasury bond futures) a bull spread is structured just the opposite, i.e., by buying a nearby month and selling a more deferred month.

Spreaders who expect stock prices to fall, would use what is known as a BEAR SPREAD. In a declining market, deferred contract months usually fall more rapidly than nearby contract months. So a bear spread involves buying a nearby month contract and selling a distant month contract. Example: the trader buys one June index future and sells one December index future at a differential of 1.50. Assuming the market declines, the spread between the June/December contracts widens to a differential of 2.00; a net spread profit is generated (.50 x $500 = $250 profit).

MAJOR MARKET INDEX (traded at the Chicago Board of Trade)

The 20 blue chip stock construction of the Major Market Index is an added advantage for investors and corporations who are seeking profit opportunities that entail less risk than outright speculative positions. The construction of the Major Market Index (MMI) often leads the other broad based indices in a market turn. As a result, many traders are buying the MMI futures at the

140

beginning of an expected market upturn and selling one of the broader based indices in anticipation of the spread widening in favor of the MMI. Traders who are expecting a market downturn are selling the MMI and buying one of the broader based indices.

Sample Spread Margins: (these depend on contract value, market volatility and brokerage house policy)

Ratio - 7:2 - MMI vs. S&P 500   - $600
Ratio - 4:1 - MMI vs. Value Line   - $1000
Ratio - 3:2 - MMI vs. S&P 500   - $200
Ratio - 2:1 - MMI vs. NYFE/NYSE   - $350

As an example of a stock index Intermarket Spread, assume a trader forecasts a bull market and expects the MMI to gain on the NYSE Composite. He buys two December MMI futures and sells one NYSE Composite contract . . .

MMI Future	NYSE Composite Future	Spread
NOW:		
Buys 2 Dec. MMI contracts at 524.30	Sells 1 Dec. NYSE Composite contract at 188.40	335.90
LATER:		
Sells 2 Dec. MMI contracts at 532.50	Buys 1 Dec. NYSE Composite contract at 193.65	338.85
RESULT:		
8.20 point gain x $250 x 2 = $4,100 (gain)	5.25 point loss x $500 = $2,625 (loss)	2.95 point gain x $500 = $1,475 (profit)

SPREAD SCOPE INC. STOCK AND FUTURES PRICE INDICES

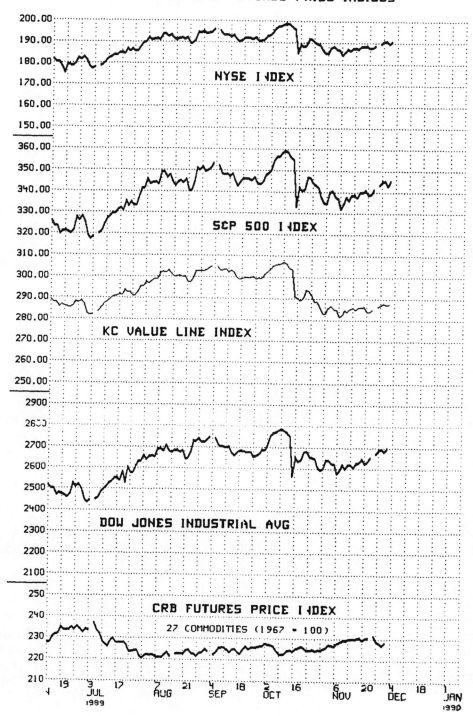

Chart courtesy of Spread Scope, Inc.

142

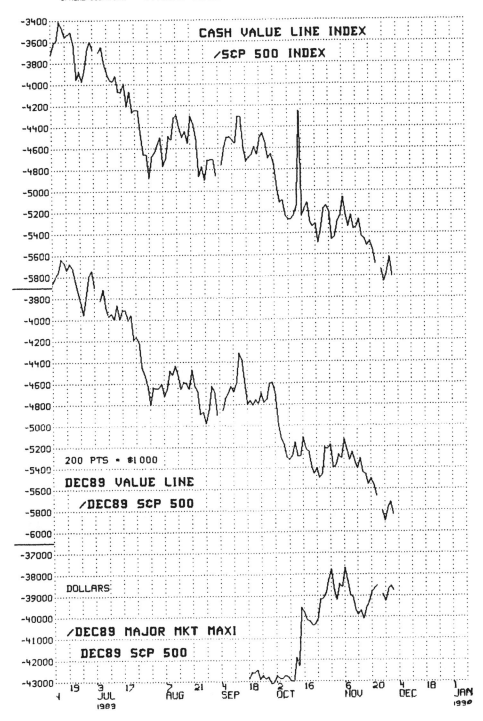

SPREAD SCOPE INC. VALUE LINE/STANDARD & POORS 500

CASH VALUE LINE INDEX
/S&P 500 INDEX

200 PTS = $1000

DEC89 VALUE LINE
/DEC89 S&P 500

DOLLARS

/DEC89 MAJOR MKT MAXI
DEC89 S&P 500

Chart courtesy of Spread Scope, Inc.

143

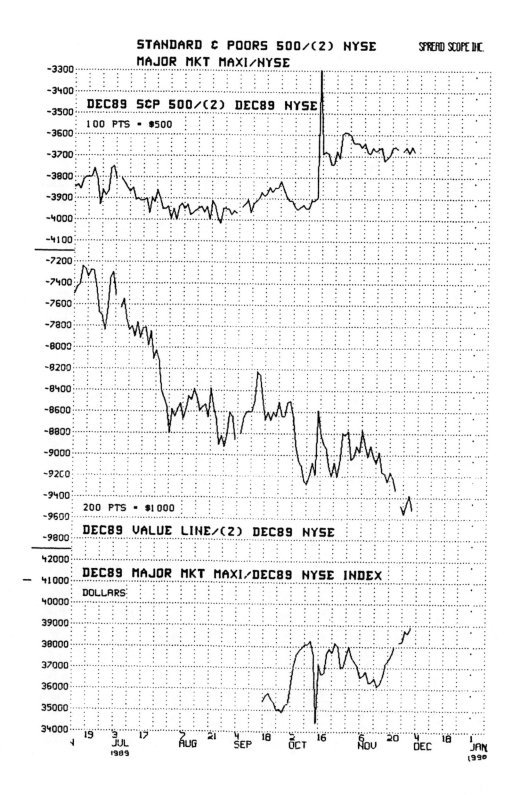

STANDARD & POORS 500/(2) NYSE   SPREAD SCOPE INC.
MAJOR MKT MAXI/NYSE

DEC89 S&P 500/(2) DEC89 NYSE

100 PTS = $500

200 PTS = $1000

DEC89 VALUE LINE/(2) DEC89 NYSE

DEC89 MAJOR MKT MAXI/DEC89 NYSE INDEX

DOLLARS

Chart courtesy of Spread Scope, Inc.

144

APPENDIX

EXPLANATORY NOTES FOR
THE SPREAD CHARTS

Dates on the charts are Mondays; data are plotted through Thursday of each week.

For intracommodity spreads, the spread difference is always the price of the nearer month minus the more distant month. For example, Dec/Mch means the price of the December contract minus the price of the March contract is plotted.

The dollar value corresponding to the spacing between the grid lines is given for each intracommodity spread and for those intercommodity and intermarket spreads involving contracts of equal size (e.g., 2¢ = $100, 50 pts = $300, etc.)

The spreads involving treasury bonds and treasury notes (both intracommodity and intercommodity) are in 32nds.

The Silver/Gold, 2 Platinum/Gold and Intercurrency spreads that involve the British pound have the difference between the total contract values (in dollars) plotted.

The crack spread has the price of 3 contracts of crude oil subtracted from the price of 1 contract of heating oil and 2 contracts of gasoline. The scale is dollars per barrel.

The carrying charges are calculated using the closing prices (nearest contract of the spread), the current bank prime interest rate plus 1%, plus fixed costs for storage and insurance. For example, $2 (2 pts) per contract per month for Gold; $7.50 (15 pts) per contract per month for Silver (as of November 1989). There is an additional one time handling charge of 20 pts for copper.

***

Charts were provided by: SPREAD SCOPE INC.
                             P.O. Box 5841
                             Mission Hills, CA 91345

147

SOME CONTRACT FACTS AND FIGURES

FINANCIALS

British Pound (IMM); 25,000 pounds; $ per pound
Canadian Dollar (IMM); 100,000 C. dollar; $ per C. dollar
Japanese Yen (IMM); 12.5 million yen; $ per yen
Swiss Franc (IMM); 125,000 francs; $ per franc
W. German Mark (IMM); 125,000 marks; $ per mark
Eurodollar, 3-mo. (IMM); $1 million; pts. of 100%;
U.S. Treasury Bills (IMM); $1 million; pts. of 100%
U.S. Treasury Bonds (CBT); 8% - $100,000 prin; pts & 32nds of 100%
10-yr. U.S. Treasury Notes (CBT); $100,000 prin; pts & 32nds of 100%

METALS

Copper (COMEX)	25,000 lb.;	¢ per lb.
Gold (COMEX)	100 troy oz.;	$ per troy oz.
Silver (COMEX)	5,000 troy oz.;	¢ per troy oz.
Silver (CBT)	1,000 troy oz.;	¢ per troy oz.
Platinum (NYME)	50 troy oz.;	$ per troy oz.
Palladium (NYME)	100 troy oz.;	$ per troy oz.

ENERGY COMPLEX

Unleaded Gas (NYME)	42,000 gal.	¢ per gal.
No. 2 Heating Oil (NYME)	42,000 gal.	¢ per gal.
Crude Oil (NYME)	1,000 bbl.	$ per bbl.
Propane Gas (NYME)	42,000 gal.	¢ per gal.

INDEX FUTURES

Muni Bond Index (CBT)	$1,000 x index; pts. & 32nds of 100%
Major Market Index-Muni (CBT)	$250 x index number
NYSE Composite Index (NYFE)	$500 x index number
Commodity Res. Bureau Index (NYFE)	$500 x index number
S&P 500 Stock Index (CME)	$500 x index number
Value Line Stock Index (KCBT)	$500 x index number
U.S. Dollar Index (FINEX)	$500 x US$ index
European Currency Unit (FINEX)	100,000 ECU Units
European Currency Units (IMM)	125,000 ECU Units

SPREAD MARGIN REQUIREMENTS (At Press Time)

Commodity:	Price Quoted In:	Initial:	Maintenance:
Copper (COMEX)	¢/lb.	$1,700	$1,700
Gold (COMEX)	$/oz.	400	300
Platinum (NYME)	$/oz.	600	500
Silver (COMEX)	¢/oz.	500	400
Pound Sterling (IMM)	$/BP	400	300
Canadian Dollar (IMM)	$/CD	400	300
Japanese Yen (IMM)	¢/JY	400	300
Swiss Franc (IMM)	$/SF	400	300
Deutsche Mark (IMM)	$/DM	400	300
Unleaded Gas (NYME)	¢/gal.	600	500
No. 2 Heating Oil (NYME)	¢/gal.	600	400
Crude Oil (NYME)	$/bbl.	600	400
Propane (NYME)	¢/gal.	200	140
European Currency Unit (IMM)	¢/ECU	——	—-
Eurodollars (NYME)	% pts.	Market	Market
GNMA Mortgage (CBT)	——	——	——
U.S. Treasury Bonds (CBT)	% pts.	Market	Market
U.S. Treasury Notes 5 Yr. (CBT)	% pts.	Market	Market
U.S. Treasury Notes 10 Yr. (CBT)	% pts.	Market	Market
U.S. Treasury Bills (IMM)	% pts.	Market	Market
Major Market Maxi (CBT)	Index pts.	Market	Market
S&P 500 Index (CME)	Index pts.	375	250
NYSE Composite Index (NYFE)	Index pts.	1,000	700
CRB Index (NYFE)	Index pts.	700	400
KC Value Line Index (KCBT)	Index pts.	1,500	1,100
Municipal Bond Index (CBT)	Index pts.	Market	Market

KEY TO CONTRACT MONTHS

First Year:	Month:	Second Year:	First Year:	Month:	Second Year:
F	Jan	A	N	Jly	L
G	Feb	B	Q	Aug	O
H	Mch	C	U	Sep	P
J	Apr	D	V	Oct	R
K	May	E	X	Nov	S
M	Jne	I	Z	Dec	T

ENTERING A SPREAD ORDER

When entering a spread order be very specific!

(1)   Make sure that the phone clerk clearly understands that you are entering a spread order: Say, "I have a spread order to enter."

(2)   Speak slowly and distinctly: Say, "Fifteen - one five" or "Fifty - five zero." When you refer to the contract months, September and December are easy to misunderstand. Say, instead: "Sep" and "Dec". Or say: "Sep like Labor Day" or "Dec like Christmas."

(3)   All orders are considered to be day orders (they will expire at the end of the trading day if not filled) unless you specify otherwise.

(4)   Spell your name and give your account number to the phone clerk.

(5)   Give the individual legs of the spread - "BUY 3 Dec 1989 IMM T-bills, SELL 3 June 1990 IMM T-bills, as a spread of 20 points or more June" (meaning that June is trading 20 points over the December contract or more).

(6)   Note in above (#5) that you always enter the buy side first, then the sell side.

(7)   Ask the phone clerk to repeat the order back to you, including the order ticket number.

(8)   When the clerk calls you back with your fill, note down his report and then repeat to him what you just wrote down.

(9)   Spreads involving Municipal bonds over Treasury bond futures (MOB), and spreads involving Treasury note futures over Treasury bond futures (NOB), are always entered by giving the spread differential in 32nds. Before entering your spreads for financial contracts, remember to convert the differential from points to 32nds. Also important to remember that with MOBs and NOBs the differential is always given to the munis (or notes), whether it is at a premium or discount. For example, if munis are trading one point under bonds (this is a negative spread), then the differential is -32/32nds.